Threadbared

Thread**bared**

Decades of Don'ts from the Sewing and Crafting World

By Mary Watkins & Kimberly Wrenn

 THREE RIVERS PRESS · NEW YORK

Published in the United States by Three Rivers Press, an
imprint of the Crown Publishing Group, a division of
Random House, Inc., New York.
www.crownpublishing.com

Three Rivers Press and the Tugboat design are registered
trademarks of Random House, Inc.

Library of Congress Cataloging-in-Publication Data
Watkins, Mary
    Threadbared : decades of don'ts from the sewing and
crafting world / by Mary Watkins and Kimberly Wrenn.
    1. Knitting—Humor.   2. Sewing—Humor.
3. Vintage clothing—Humor.   I. Wrenn, Kimberly,
1974–   II. Title.
    TT820.W285   2006
    746.02'07—dc22   2006013889

ISBN-13: 978-0-307-34207-2
ISBN-10: 0-307-34207-7

Printed in the United States of America

Design by Kay Schuckhart / Blond on Pond

10 9 8 7 6 5 4 3 2 1

First Edition

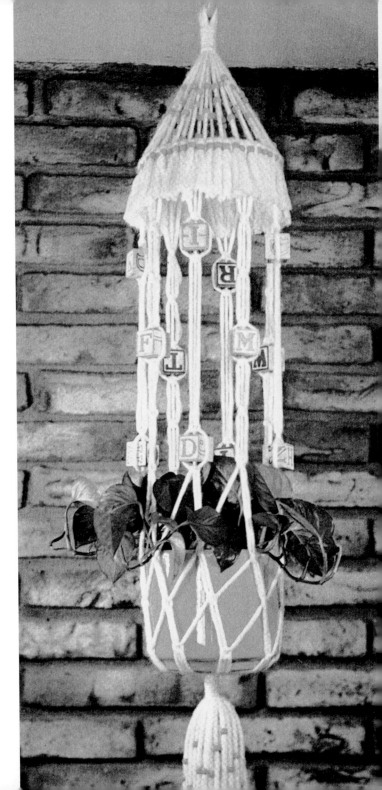

To all the readers of Threadbared.com

Contents

Fair and Warmer
the fascinator with the
eye-eye appeal

Introduction

Since the dawn of time, pattern companies have been churning out directions for constructing "fabulous" apparel and crafts right in the comfort of one's own home. (OK . . . maybe not since the dawn of time. Maybe more like 100 years or so . . . but "dawn of time" sounds so dramatic.) Ranging from delicate drawings of designer gowns to photos of shiny-faced knitwear models, these patterns serve as markers for what our society generously calls fashion.

While some people with a fondness for vintage wear might use these patterns to actually *make* dresses, sweaters, culottes, or panties, your humble authors have an unfortunate inability to sew, knit, crochet, or do anything even remotely crafty.

Thus, we turn to our vast supply of sarcasm. Instead of making things, we make *fun* of things.

We know what you're thinking: Who are these girls and what qualifies them to be so catty and mocking? Sadly, the latter question has no good answer, but we can help you out with that first one.

Growing up in the South, we were taught three basic rules: Nice girls don't make fun of others, nice girls don't curse, and nice girls don't wear open-toed shoes in December.

Unfortunately, we loved to do all three.

A native of Macon, Georgia, Kimberly Wrenn grew up with a father who preached for a living and a mother who sewed everything for her, from adorable smocked dresses to a slutty-French-maid Halloween costume. And '80s dresses, complete with the big butt bow. But after Kimberly was forced to make what turned out to be the world's most hideous pink teddy-bear pillow while in Home Economics, it became clear that she would never fill her mother's talented and productive shoes. Years later, while studying psychology, she discovered that the only things that truly interested her were those that inspired the phrase "ooohhh . . . pretty." Thus, she found herself collecting charming old sewing patterns. Patterns she had no idea what to do with.

A few miles over, in LaGrange, Mary Watkins avoided Home Ec and rolled her eyes when her mother suggested she sew a button. *(Hello? Women's liberation anyone?)* But after college she made a most startling discovery. This whole "career" thing was vastly overrated. Work was hard and business suits sucked. She longed for a simpler time, and began to take an unwholesome interest in the (very wholesome) '50s. She filled her home with midcentury furniture and stocked her linen closet with vintage aprons. She even snagged a husband who was willing to use a rotary phone. She may have missed out on the golden era of domesticity, but it was never too late to catch up.

Then Mary and Kimberly moved to Atlanta, met each other, and all hell broke loose.

We discovered a number of common interests: sweet tea with bourbon, at-home hair-coloring experiments, handbags we could never afford, and vintage fashions long abandoned by others. Only when we looked more closely at our collection of vintage patterns did we discover that they weren't just fetching. They were, well . . . hilarious.

Together we set out to answer perplexing questions about these vintage patterns, such as:

- What's the deal with all those men wearing pajamas and brandishing golf clubs?
- Why are all the women's waists so damn small? Girdles? Malnutrition? *Tapeworms?*
- Does the world really *need* a crocheted clown toilet paper cover?
- Is the perfect woman really one who has a great personality *and* makes her own panties?
- And lastly, did people really make all of this stuff? And if so, did they wear it out of their houses? In *public*?

And so, with a fondness for the fashions and the values of the past, we commence making fun of people and cursing, just as we were taught never to do. Oh, and we also wrote this entire book while wearing seasonally inappropriate footwear. *The horror!*

'40s

There May Be a War Going On, but Everyone's Still Having a Gay Old Time!

Ah, the 1940s! It was a time of war, Rosie the Riveter, big band radio, zoot suits, and lots and lots of knitwear. Everyone went crazy with knitted sweaters, knitted jerkins, knitted collars, knitted hats, knitted handbags, knitted mittens, knitted scarves, knitted socks, knitted baby clothes, knitted playsuits, knitted toys, and finally, knitted knitting baskets to hold knitting materials.

We're sure that there was some sewing going on, but we didn't find it. As far as we can tell, the '40s enforced a strict knitting-only craft policy.

Hey, they had to improvise back then—the country was at war and fabric availability was limited. Today, a cloth shortage would merely result in a widespread movement of Americans wearing patriotic pasties and G-strings, but people were a wee bit more conservative back in the 1940s.

Well, okay, we *thought* they were more conservative. But we could have been wrong, because we were stunned over and over again by the surplus of "gay" clothing articles touted in the mid-'40s. If you weren't buttoning up your gay cardigan sweater, then you were likely topping off your outfit with a gay little beanie.

All in all, it was an interesting era for pattern makers. With fabric scarce and the men sent off to war, most American women were sewing their family's apparel, and even finding new uses for it. Some companies produced patterns for transforming men's suits into ladies' suits and women's dresses into children's clothing. Others tried to market patterns that would alter children's clothing into men's suits and dogs' sweaters into ladies' hats, but those never really sold quite as well.

And thus concludes our brief introduction to patterns of the 1940s. Now, everyone go put on a knitted sweater or a gay beanie and *let's get started!*

Thurston Howell III: The Early Years

E ver wonder what Thurston Howell was like as an eight-year-old?

So, I said, "Mummy, that's not a yacht, that's a dinghy!" HAH!

Anyway, Gregory, as I was saying before . . . you need to diversify your portfolio; the energy sector is frightfully passé. Look into the Asian markets, old chap; that's where the future lies. Daddy was just saying the other day that . . .

Gregory? Gregory, you're not listening to a word I'm saying, are you? Hmmm? Gregory?

Oh, forget it . . . let's just go feed caviar to the dog again!

Donning Now Our Gay Apparel

When you think 1944, you think conservative Christian beliefs, traditional American values, and so on. Right?

Think again, folks, think again.

The 1940s was such a progressive time that even *knitting booklets* pushed a provocative, nonconformist agenda for the teenagers of the day. If Jerry Falwell had been alive at the time, he would have died and then rolled over in his grave.*

Ladies and gentlemen, we present "Gay Teen Ideas."

Oh sure, sure . . . it doesn't seem so shocking *now*. Keep in mind, though—this pamphlet was published before MTV, before *The Rocky Horror Picture Show* . . . hell, it was even before k. d. lang.

While every same-sex preference isn't represented—the booklet relies largely on a "lipstick lesbianism" role—it's still surprisingly advanced for its time. We have to warn you, Gentle Readers, some of these "teen ideas" are just a little shocking, a little arresting, just a little bit ahead of their time. Don't say we didn't warn you.

*Oh wait, he *was* alive. But he was only eleven. So . . . never mind.

Gay Teen Idea #1

W e're here to tell you . . .

LISTEN, something pretty pulsating is going on. The coke crowd's going to town with its very own knitting and crocheting *Teen Fashions*, smooth and super with plenty of paprika to make those beaux' eyes blink.

W e're here to tell you . . .

LISTEN, something pretty pulsating is going on. The coke crowd's going to town with its very own knitting and crocheting *Teen Fashions*, smooth and super with plenty of paprika to make those beaux' eyes blink.
One swift look-see inside is enough to make any girl with an oz. of get-up-and-go in her veins take to her needles. Want a ski outfit that'll make you Queen of the Snow Carnival? Try your hand at Chilly Sauce on page 12. Looking for some glamour-drama? The P.M. sweater on page 15 is your dish. Get a load of the New-some Two-some jerkin and beanie that'll make you a *Scenic Distraction!* Talking about scenery, *Here's looking at You* (page 11) gives you some hot clues on how to improve your own. Try the *fashion quiz* and get hep to who's going with who in the Gadget Gallery. A couple of skeins of yarn and strict attention to the Directions in the back of the book and take a look, you're an Eyeful for merely a Trifle!

W hat in the hell is going on here?

Something *pulsating*? The *coke* crowd? Plenty of *paprika* in the eyes??? Are the Gay Teens on DRUGS?

One swift look-see inside is enough to make any girl with an oz. of get-up-and-go in her veins take to her needles.

Veins?

Needles???

Oh, sweet Christ, the Gay Teens are chasing the dragon! *What next?*

Gay Teen Idea #2

Calf love? *Calf love???* Good Lord, these teens are into positively *everything!*

Is nothing safe anymore? First, they start with the Calf Love; next thing you know, they're moving on to Elbow Eroticism and . . . and . . . and then what? Armpit Amour? *Inner-Ear Intimacy?* Oh, we don't want to know.

Hot hot hot!!! Barely legal calves!

feet first

● Toes Toasties—so nice to come home to. Cozy "after-ski" slippers, but there's no law against using them for just plain cold feet.

● The Long and Short of It—ankles away in a snazzy pair of socks. If you keep right on knitting chances are it'll be a good case of *calf love.*

● Slipper, slipper, who's got the slipper? The first thing in the A.M., the last thing in the P.M., these two will be your favorite standbys.

● Follow the leader. It's a smart dog that knows his dogs. He can tell a good thing when he sees it, couldn't you?

Directions on page 20

Directions on page 21

No. 2053

No.

Directions on page 21

No. 2061

Directions on page 27

DizzyMaking

Oₕ, what a beautiful feelin'! The sun is shinin', the band is playin' and you're right on the beam in your jerkin that keeps 'em perkin'.

No. 2050

Directions for making page 20

Oₕ, what a beautiful feelin'! The sun is shinin', the band is playin' and you're right on the beam in your jerkin that keeps 'em perkin'. Two are always more fun than one, so there's a dilly of a beanie to match. P.S. If the ride doesn't make him dizzy, you'll be sure to turn his head faster than you can say *giddap-and-go!*

4

You're right on the beam in your jerkin that keeps 'em perkin'?

Huh.

We knew a girl in high school whose jerkin' was supposed to keep them perkin', but she still didn't get a date for the senior prom, so I'd say that's not really enough to get the boys' attention after all.

Anyway, *boys*? What's with the boys? Where are the Gay Teens we were promised? So far this booklet is all talk and no action. This reader does not just ask but *demands,* "Bring on the Gay Teens already!"

Gay Teen Idea #4

Oh. Okay. There they are. Ginger on the left is rather alluring in a haughty, bitchy sort of way (*rrrrow!*), and Plain June over on the right is understandably aroused. She thinks Ginger's just the *keenest*, even if she did christen June with the nickname "Tin Lezzie" after June stuffed all those poems through the slats in Ginger's locker. The other girls at school teased June for weeks after that—all except Winifred Williams, who asked if she wanted to join a Secret Sapphic Society, to which June had to politely decline, as she doesn't have time for any other extracurricular activities since she's already captain of the Girls' Bowling Team, the Girls' Softball Team, and the Girls' Arm-Wrestling Team. Plus, there's all that time spent hiding underneath the bleachers watching Ginger at cheerleading practice. Besides, the *Sapphic Society*? Please. June isn't even *taking* Latin this term.

Despite all the obstacles, June remains undeterred; she knows that Ginger is her soul mate and that eventually she'll come around. After all, how could she resist June's pretty, pretty pearls and calf-lovin' socks?

Gay Teen Idea #5

Time to Be Pretty

No. 2055

FASCINATIN' baby with those sweet beguilin' ways . . . perfectly irresistible, this lacy wool mantilla. It takes no time to make and makes you so lovely to look at.

Directions on page 22

10

Whether you're a Ginger or a June, every Gay Teen wants to be pretty. This was 1944, after all, long before the age of multiple body piercings, oversized plaid flannel shirts, and crew cuts for girls. No, in the 1940s it was Lipstick Lesbianism or no lesbianism at all.

But just how do you know what to do when it's Time to Be Pretty? Sure, you could consult your best pal, older sister, mom, or current popular fashion magazine. But "Gay Teen Ideas" is there for you, too, covering all the bases. Amid instructions for knitted mittens and cardigan sweaters, the booklet includes a rather inexplicable selection of beauty, exercise, and diet tips.

How 'bout a sample, you ask? Sure thing. Here's a little excerpt on an all-important topic: the necessity of a little thing called P-O-I-S-E.

> Let's start with that prize possession, P-O-I-S-E. It's one part being sure of yourself and that comes from good grooming—omit pins in the hem, thank you, snow-white collar, shining, clean brushed hair, a lovely, clean, fragrant smell (deodorant dept, please note!). The other part is knowing how to stand and walk. Most people haven't learned the simple art of holding their spines straight, and they develop torsos that look like the bumps. Try this for size. Stand ten inches away from wall, knees slightly bent, arms at side. Lean back against wall and settle the small of your back smack against it. Now poo-osh the back of your neck against the wall, keeping chin in and down. Make sure there's no daylight between the small of your back and wall. Now slowly raise your arms straight over your head to wall and bring 'em back to your sides *without budging that back*. Repeat ten times, A.M. and P.M.

What in the H-E-L-L are they talking about? Pins in the hem and deodorant department aside—most people develop *"torsos that look like bumps"*? What about legs that look like stumps? Kneecaps that look like lumps? Noses that look like clumps? Breath that smells like sump pumps?

Ugh, the imagery is just getting too weird. We're going to let this one go and just poo-osh the thoughts out of our minds.

Fair and Warmer the fascinator with the eye-eye appeal

Directions on page 28

Here's looking at you . . .

WHATEVER nature dished out to you in the way of looks, once you're old enough to think about them, you, and nobody but you, is responsible for the Result. You can start out with a pretty sweet chassis and end up, thanks to poor diet, no exercise and slovenly grooming, in the droopy dept. On the other hand you can begin with a skimpy beauty capital and turn yourself into an honest-to-goodness self-made Cutie. Just don't expect a fairy godmother to come around with a magic wand and do it *for* you. You'll have to do it all by your sweet determined little self and what's more, keep at it as regular as eating.

LET's start with that prize possession, P-O-I-S-E. It's one part being sure of yourself and that comes from good grooming—omit pins in the hem, thank you, snow white collar, shining, clean brushed hair, a lovely, clean, fragrant smell (deodorant dept, please note!). The other part is knowing how to stand and walk. Most people haven't learned the simple art of holding their spines straight, and they develop torsos that look like the bumps. Try this for size. Stand ten inches away from wall, knees slightly bent, arms at side. Lean back against wall and settle the small of your back smack against it. Now poo-osh the back of your neck against the wall, keeping chin in and down. Make sure there's no daylight between the small of your back and wall. Now slowly raise your arms straight over your head to wall and bring 'em back to your sides *without budging that back*. Repeat ten times, A.M. and P.M.

PLEASE remember that health equals beauty. Anybody can tell by looking at you if you're a lots-of-green-salad, plenty-of-fruit-milk-and-eggs gal or the fancy-dessert-and-candy type. If your waistline doesn't give you away, your skin will. Want to glow all over and make other people glow at sight of you? Want all the nice happy things of life to come your way naturally? Want to make it easy for people to like you? Remember it doesn't happen unless you *make* it happen. And remember *it can happen!* What are you waiting for?

CATHIE WELLS

Gay Teen Idea #6

Gay by Day Right by Night

This gay little sweater is inspired by the brightly colored boleros beloved by gypsies. Wear it today with slacks or a sport skirt . . . wear it tonight with a long, swishing evening skirt. You will make a dent in the stag line at the beach or at the country club dance. It's new, it's fun to make.

MIDRIFF SWEATER
Size 12-14

Materials Required—
AMERICAN THREAD COMPANY
"DAWN" SHETLAND FLOSS.

5 1-oz. Balls, Red or any color desired.

2 1-oz. Balls, White.

1 Pr. No. 1 Needles.

1 Pr. No. 3 Needles, Bone Crochet Hook No. 2 or No. 3.

Gauge—7 sts = 1 inch.   12 pattern rows = 1 inch.

Measurements: Across back 12 inches.

Underarm seam 7½ inches.

Sleeve 2½ inches.

Pattern: With White, K 1 row, P 1 row, K 1 row, P 1 row.

Attach Red, K 2 rows, P 1 row, K 1 row, pick up White and repeat from beginning.

With Red on No. 1 needles, cast on 108 sts and work in ribbing of K 2, P 2, for 1½ inches, change to No. 3 needles and work in pattern until work measures 7 inches from beginning.

Next 8 Rows—Bind off 4 sts at the beginning of each row then decrease 1 st at beginning of each row 8 times. Work even until armhole measures 6½ inches.

Next 10 Rows—Bind off 6 sts at beginning of each row and bind off remaining sts for back of neck.

LEFT FRONT. Cast on 58 sts and work same as back to underarm.

Next Row—Bind off 4 sts at the beginning of row for armhole.

Next Row—Decrease 1 st at neck edge.

Next Row—Decrease 1 st at armhole edge, then decrease 1 st at armhole every other row 3 more times and decrease 1 st at neck edge every 4th row 17 more times then decrease at neck edge every 3rd row twice.

Next Row—Bind off 6 sts at armhole side for shoulder work 1 row even, repeat the last 2 rows 3 times, bind off remaining 6 sts.

Work other front to correspond reversing the armhole shaping.

SLEEVE. On No. 1 needles with Red cast on 76 sts and work in ribbing of K 2, P 2, for 1½ inches.

Change to No. 3 needles and work in stockinette st of K 1 row, P 1 row for 1 inch.

Next 2 Rows—Bind off 4 sts at the beginning of each row.

Next Row—Decrease 1 st at each end then decrease 1 st at each end every 4th row 7 more times, then decrease 1 st at each and every 3rd row 14 times, work 2 rows even, bind off remaining 24 sts.

Sew seams and sew sleeves in position.

Work 6 rows of s c up each side of front to decreasing point working 2 s c in each Red stripe and skipping to White stripe (measuring 4 inches). Work 2 rows s c around the entire neck line. Sew 4 inch zipper in front as illustrated.

[13]

A nd thus concludes our peek into the exciting world of Gay Teen Ideas.

You know, when you start to think about it, who says we're really so open-minded in 2006? Oh *sure,* we love the Gay Teens when they're kissing each other on *The O.C.,* and yet we continue exploiting them on "coming out" episodes of *The Maury Povich Show* and sending them off to deprogramming camps in scenic Utah.

Open-minded, indeed.

At least in 1944 a Gay Teen could just *be* a Gay Teen, a person in her own right. Hey, if *knitting pamphlets* were okay with it, then *everybody* was okay with it, right?

I think we've all learned a little something here today. Something about acceptance. About equality. About sweaters.

But mostly acceptance and equality. Oh, and we also learned exercises for torsos that look like bumps. Although frankly, we still don't know what the hell *that* was about.

Disturbing Lyrics Brought to You by Barnes & Barnes, Circa 1982

Kid heads kid heads
Roly-poly kid heads

Kid heads kid heads
Eat them up
Yum!

5320

5321

5322

5323
(Directions on
page 31)

Speak to Us, O Spirits of the Strip Club

"Speak to us, Mighty Spirits of the crystal ball. Speak to us of things that are and things that will come to be. Tell us, O Wise Ones . . . what will Krissy's profession be when she grows up?"

"Do you see anything?"

"Wait, I do see something—it looks like a list of instructions. It says: Do these things and your future profession will be clear."

"I'm so excited! Read me the instructions."

"OK. It says: First take off your skirt. Then swing it over your head."

"Gotcha. What's next?"

"Kick off your stilettos and swivel your hips around and around."

"Like this?"

"I guess so. Now it says toss the skirt at the nearest man."

"OK, but I'm not getting this. What do you think it all means? What will I be when I grow up?"

"I'm not sure. But I'm guessing you'll need a stage name and some pasties."

Threadbared Presents: Things That Will Get Your Son's Ass Kicked

#1. The demure and very ladylike hand-anchored leg cross. You can't see it, but just out of the frame, this little nancy boy's foot is swinging in tiny genteel circles.

#2. Wearing a flowery sweater that exactly matches the flowery sweater of your sister, with whom you walk around *holding hands*. (And we're not even bothering to mention the kiddie comb-over and ongoing game of pocket pool.)

#3. A beret. A beret is a guaran-damn-teed ass-kicking. Look at that kid. He's trying to be upbeat, but he knows he's getting a swirlie after recess.

#4. A ginormous potato head and Tyrannosaurus rex arms. The five-inch camel toe won't help to ward off the milk money thieves, either.

#5. Standing like *this*. Even the little girl in the back with her tushie hanging out of her skirt can't help but laugh at him.

So mommies beware. Sending your precious punkins out into the world sporting any of these ass-kickable fashions is giving him a one-way ticket to Wedgie-ville.

Oh, Men's Sweaters. Is There Anything You *Can't* Do?

BOOK NO. 240

10¢

Men's Sweaters

Chadwick's RED HEART Wools

No. 404
Page 22

At last—an uncensored, in-depth look into the world of Men's Sweaters!

Oh, like you haven't been curious for years now! Like you haven't asked yourself time and time again, "Sure, I know that men need sweaters. We *all* need sweaters. But tell me more! Is there really a need for different types of sweaters for different types of men? Aren't they all pretty much the *same*?"

Well, let's take a look, shall we?

Ah, the Young Modern! He's an intellectual, a world traveler, the type of man who annoyingly refers to himself as a real "Renaissance Man."

Only a funnel-neck pullover will do. It's young. It's modern. It's a real Renaissance Sweater.

Streamlined
Design

No. 402...36 – 38 – 40 – 42

Look at Mr. Streamlined Design and his T-square. He looks a bit uptight, but frankly we're not too concerned with him (and his streamlined sweater vest). No, we're much more interested in the cartoon man with the looooooong sports car. He seems to be . . . uh . . . *overcompensating* for something, don't you think?

For those insecure in their manhood—V-neck vests: the only way to go!

Executive Material

No. 401...38 – 40 – 42 – 44

The Executive Material man—he's a real success story. And nothing screams "success" quite like a button-down cardigan sweater.

Looking at the photo, you can almost hear all the enterprising young whippersnappers at the office falling all over themselves to compliment him.

"Say, Mr. Johnson, that's a swell *sweater you're wearing today!"*

"Yessir, nobody wears a sweater quite like you, Mr. Johnson!"

Good Mixer

No. 410 . . . Sizes 36 – 38 – 40 – 42

Finally, we round things out with this young smoothie, also known as the Good Mixer. Just what makes him such a good mixer?

Well, obviously, let's look first at his sweater. This little V-neck number is knitted with a synthetic blend, so spilled martinis merely "wick away" rather than soak in. It's fire-retardant, so any dropped cigarettes won't cause a panic. And of course, the V-neck design lends itself to bow tie wearing, and everyone knows that girls can't resist a man with a bow tie. The Good Mixer also has a trust fund, a Rolls-Royce, and his own private tennis court, and is rumored to have genitalia rivaling that of the legendary Milton Berle . . . but that seems beside the point.

Clearly, his success lies in his choice of sweater.

Oh, Men's Sweaters, what would we do without you?

I Just Hope I Don't End Up in One of Those Dreadful Preschools Where They Send People to Die

You may ask yourself, "Why is this baby dressed like an 85-year-old woman? Why the granny sweater and that old-lady cap that Charlie's grandma Josephine wore in *Charlie and the Chocolate Factory*?" Well, allow me to enlighten you, my ignorant friend.

This baby is part of the "regressing is the new aging" movement. It's sweeping the nation. No. Seriously. It is. This baby will begin her life wearing orthopedic shoes and poufy bonnets. Then she'll move on to control-top panty hose and jewelry that's just slightly too large. After a brief time spent in the dreaded twinset, she'll transition to mom jeans and holiday-themed sweaters with bells, whistles, pulleys, and levers all over them. Somewhere around age 60, she'll spend hours searching for just the right pair of work slacks and the perfect little black dress. Then she'll head directly to low-rise jeans and T-shirts with funny slogans. By the time she's 85, she'll be sporting onesies with tiny puppies all over them. When you think about it, it's the perfect plan. I mean, she'll be the only one with a less embarrassing explanation for the diapers.

Puff crowns for cream puffs

I'll See Your Cankle and Raise You One Love Handle

Hey! That saleslady was right. The box pleats DO make my ass look smaller! Now, if only I could do something about these damn cankles and find an undershirt that lifts and separates.

Triple-Testicled Toboggan

Here Is Where We Rib You

Oh yes, here is, indeed, where we rib you.

We rib you for your Jovi Chick bangs sprouting from the front of your hat. We rib you for the Tootsie Roll curls leaping precociously from the back.

We rib you for your triple-testicled volcano toboggan.

We do admire the redundant pent-up-energy symbolism, but really, two testicles would have been enough to make your point.

THE '50s

Golly Gee, What a Swell Era! Now, if Only We Could Breathe...

In 1947, Dior introduced the "New Look," thus changing fashion for the following decade. The dresses represented a classic femininity, and after the fabric scrimping of the '40s, everyone was eager to indulge with yards and yards of fabric for the skirts.

Heck, we love the clothes from the 1950s. The full skirts, the intricate details, not to mention those fabulous 15-inch waists! How the women breathed back then is a wonder to us, but gee, they sure did look great trying.

The men's clothing...well, it wasn't nearly as pretty, but it wasn't bad, either. This was the age of The Gray Flannel Suit, and men marched around in droves wearing them. Forget black, navy, and dark brown suits—those smacked of communism and you didn't want to cause any suspicions. Men also wore hats in the '50s. Not sometimes. Not most of the time. All the time. Even to bed. Even in the bath. And let me tell you, it's a real bitch trying to shampoo your hair while wearing a fedora.

What about those peachy-keen teens of the decade? Contrary to popular belief, no self-respecting teenager in the 1950s looked like a cast member from *Grease*. Sure, they wore the same flouncy dresses as their mothers (with the same scratchy petticoats underneath), but they were a little more conservative than the likes of Sandra Dee. And the one guy at the high school who looked like Fonzie...well, he was just bad news.

Of course, the '50s were also home to the beatnik generation. But there's really only so much you can say about a black turtleneck, dig?

Due to an Unfortunate Cropping Incident with a Local Art Director, Danny Is Represented As a Triple Amputee on His Very First Catalog Cover

"Ah, Rolf, yes, yes . . . come in. We were just looking at your cover for this month's knitting booklet and, well . . . there's a problem. The lighting looks swell and we loved the props you used; that little airplane—so cute! But . . . well . . . it seems like you've cropped little Danny's legs right off at the knees. Nobody's gonna want to buy a pattern book featuring a kid with no shins."

"Well, that's true. We are selling patterns for sweaters and not pants. But now that you mention it . . . it sort of looks like little Danny's missing an arm as well. . . ."

"Rolf . . . Rolf. *Calm down, Rolf.* Yes, I realize that we're selling sweaters and not right arms. . . ."

"Boy, you artsy types—such a temperament! Screw it. Let's print 'em."

Did He Just Yell "FORE"?

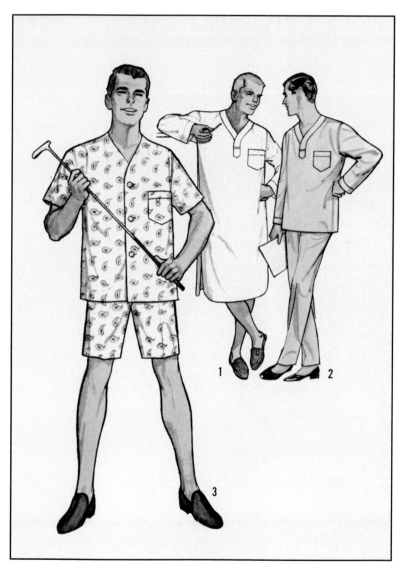

"I agree, Todd. It was swell of Bruce to invite us to his sleepover, but what the heck do you think he's planning to do with that golf club?"

These Men Love Women.
No, Seriously.

Nos 897 and 898
instructions on pages 22 and 23

The folks over at Diamond have created a fun catalog of patterns for totally 100 percent straight men. Take a look. And let me just stress one more time—these men are completely hetero.

Gee, Tom, darts are real fun, but I'd really like to jump in the hot tub. Trouble is, we only have one set of swim trunks between us. Whatever shall we do?
I tell you what, Bruce. I'll play you for the swim trunks. Loser goes *au naturel*!

Alrighty, Bruce! I have on my fairly won trunks and I have the oar you requested. Wait a second! I said *au naturel*, not all neutrals!

Nos 893 and 892 instructions on pages 18 and 15

Nos 884 and 885
instructions on pages 5 and 7

No 899
instructions on page 23

Have You Ever Asked Yourself, "Did I Possibly Give Birth to a Future Evil Dictator?"

- Does your baby repeatedly clasp his or her hands together and laugh manically?

- Was your baby's first word *"Heil!"*?

- Is your baby's favorite bedtime story *The Little Fascist That Could*?

- Does your baby's laughter have a distinct *"mmmwahahaha"* sound?

If you've answered "yes" to any of these questions, your baby could possibly be a Future Evil Dictator! No need to panic, just be sure to bring this up during your next pediatrician visit.

Before Bela Lugosi, Lon Chaney, and Boris Karloff, There Was . . . Garry

With an uneasy feeling, Billy suddenly realizes he forgot to bring his wooden cross and garlic to the photo shoot.

On a side note—Garry? G-A-R-R-Y? Did Garry's mom fail second-grade spelling? Or did Patons just goof up on their model sweater and decide to go with it?

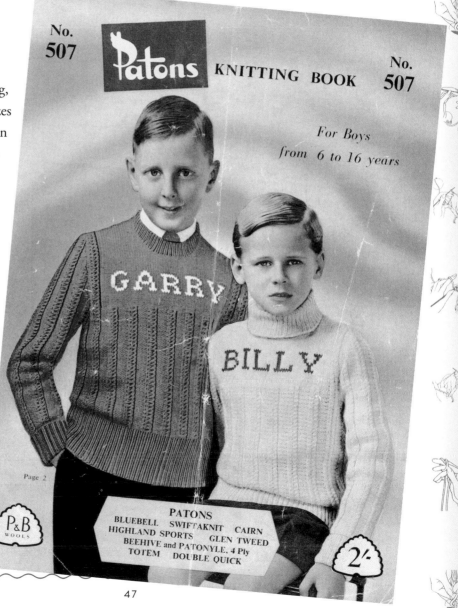

No. 507

Patons KNITTING BOOK No. 507

For Boys from 6 to 16 years

GARRY

BILLY

Page 2

P&B WOOLS

PATONS
BLUEBELL   SWIFTAKNIT   CAIRN
HIGHLAND SPORTS   GLEN TWEED
BEEHIVE and PATONYLE, 4 Ply
TOTEM   DOUBLE QUICK

2/-

Festive Stoles and Blouses—and the Bitches Who Love Them

J. & P. COATS · CLARK'S **O.N.T.** STOLES and BLOUSES BOOK No. 296 10¢

Festive **Stoles** and BLOUSES

CHADWICK'S RED ♥ HEART YARNS

Gentle Readers, do not be intimidated by the severe women on the cover of this 1952 knitting booklet—surely things aren't as unwelcoming inside.

Magic in the Moonlight

Crochet—for important evenings

Elaine S-383 (blouse above left) . . . Esther S-384 (dress above right) . . Directions on Page 10

Directions for Velveteen Stole on Page 15

·8·

Denise S-385 (blouse at right)

Directions on Page 13

Joyce C-162 (stole below)

Directions on Page 12

Rose S-386 (blouse at right)

Directions on Page 11

Oh.
Well, never mind.

Below: Those bitches have scared the hell out of poor Esther, too. Either she's terrified out of her skull or she's just not able to breathe properly at the moment . . . that rubber band around her waist seems to be cutting off her circulation. Between wheezes, she twitches and blinks, verging on a major mental collapse. Please, someone get Esther a daiquiri immediately!

Above: Elaine wears a crocheted rayon blouse and a slightly worried expression. She always thought she was rather steely, but after sizing up the dispassionate likes of Denise, Joyce, and Rose over on the other page, she has realized that she is out of her league. *Way* out of her league. She begins to slowly creep backward, trying to disappear off the page.

Above: Looking at Denise, you can just tell that she's the type of she-devil to squeeze your arm and call you "Daaaarling" to your face but to secretly refer to you as "Prize Heifer" when her Junior League pals are around and you're not. Denise's motto is "You Can Never Be Too Rich or Too Thin, But You Had Sure as Hell Better Not Be Richer or Thinner Than I Am." Seriously. You saw it embroidered on a throw pillow in her front lounge one time.

Below: Joyce has an Evil Eyebrow that really seems to say it all:

"I *own* you backbiting hags, so DON'T EVEN START WITH ME."

When the Eyebrow speaks, you can *bet* that everybody damn sure listens.

Rose clearly relies on the blood of young virgins to keep her alive. But with a fetching V-neck sweater and a festive beaded belt accentuating her 14-inch waist, you barely even notice the protruding fangs and faint traces of marrow caked in the corners of her mouth.

He Had a Whole Drawerful, Greg Had Figured—What Difference Would It Make If He Took *One*?

It was the day of the big game, and everything had gone just swell. Greg and Linda were getting ready to celebrate the victory with hamburgers and Cokes . . . when suddenly they saw him. Storming across the quad, he pointed directly at Greg and frowned. He didn't look happy. Greg gulped and hoped that Linda couldn't hear his heart pounding in his chest.

It was the Big Man On Campus, and he was looking for his missing tube sock.

"Also, Timmy, Let's Try Not to Look So . . . Um . . . Excited."

PATONS BOOK
No. 700

Boys' Wear — 6 Years to Teens — 25 to 36 ins.
PATONS TOTEM • TYROL • JET

Patons
KNITTING BOOK 700
WITH T.V. DESIGNS

2'6
25 CENTS

Okay, yes, yes . . . with your hand on his shoulder. But, Franklin, this time let's try looking a little less . . . *suggestive.*

That's it . . . that's it! Timmy, *yes*—big smiles! Franklin . . . left hand on his shoulder. Now hook your thumb in your pocket and look straight at the camera. Okay, *perfect* . . . except, Franklin, I hate to keep saying this, buddy, but *please*—not so carnal this time, okay?

Beyond Flattering in Every Way

Looking for a stylish alternative to jeans this summer? Feeling self-conscious that your figure isn't *quite right* for all the "low-rider" styles that the young people wear these days?

Look no further! MomCapris™ are a fun way to have the hot "retro" style *without* sacrificing comfort!

- Patented, adjustable UltraHigh® Waist keeps things chaste from the waist down, whether you prefer your waist directly under your armpits *or* hitting the middle of your rib cage!

- The built-in "pooch" in front features your belly prominently, whether you've gained some tummy weight or *just want to look like you have!*

- Special seams along the hips help "pad things out" for the look of a fuller figure. No need to worry about womanly curves with MomCapris™—the seams take care of it *for you!* What man doesn't love a gal with large, womanly hips?!

MomCapris™ are stain-resistant, so they're perfect for doing chores around the home. But tuck in your shirt and add some pearls and lipstick, and *voilà*—MomCapris™ are ready to hit the town! Why would you want to wear anything else?

Sadistic Catalog Photographers and the Children Who Fear Them

No. 384 **Patons** KNITTING BOOK No. 384

1/6d.

FROM 5 TO 15 YEARS

P&B WOOLS

Good Lord.

I have never seen two children look more depressed over a puppy. (Well, a *live* puppy, anyway.)

One can only imagine the dialogue whispered back and forth between these poor lads:

"Gee, Skip, I sure do like this puppy dog. He's pretty swell."

"I know it, Jimmy. But hush! You remember what the photographer man said, dontcha? If we behave extra good during today's modeling shoot, then little Scruffy will get to live."

"But if we don't? What if we *accidentally* misbehave, Skip? Huh? *What then?* You remember what he did to that soft brown bunny rabbit last month."

"Don't think about it, Jimmy. *Just don't think about it.*"

What Do You Do If You Can't Find the Perfect Family for Your "Sweaters for the Family" Booklet?

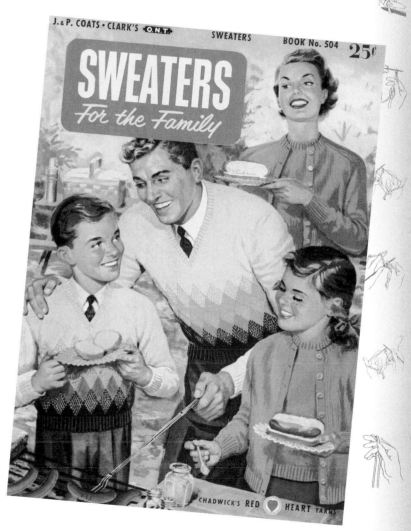

Why, you draw them, of course! Draw the sweaters, too—that way everything is bound to look good. Heck, why didn't we think of this before?

The booklet opens with this lively family scene. The theme of today? "The Family That Eats Wieners and Wears Matching Sweaters Together Stays Together!" Or something. Actually, the theme could use a little work.

Bud and Sis look fairly normal, in a kittenish sort of way, and even though Dad's a little *too* cheerful, we're not worried.

Until we take a better look at Mom and realize she's having one of her manic episodes again. Gosh, Mom, you look like you're ready to put Dad's noggin right between those buns and take a chomp on the old man's head. NO, MOM! DON'T DO IT!

Mom's prescription for Mother's Little Helper has *finally* been delivered by the pharmacy! After cooking breakfast, doing fourteen loads of laundry, vacuuming the den, bedrooms, and ceilings, transferring the cherry trees from the front yard to the back, and waxing the kitchen floor, family sedan, and golden retriever, Mom asks Bud and the others to join her for a quick game of badminton.

So far the score is Dad/Sis—0, Mom/Bud—82.

Later that day, we . . .

WAIT A MINUTE!

Who the hell are these people? And what did they do with Mom and Dad?

Either a pair of interlopers has taken over the household (sitting in Dad's chair, smoking his pipe— the *nerve!*), or Mom and Dad have decided to spice things up a bit with a couple of makeovers.

Either way, things seem to be looking up. Just look at those darling sweaters!

THE '60s

We All Put Our Sweaters on One Leg at a Time (Or Something)

Although we Threadbared gals have no direct knowledge of the '60s, we do have siblings that lived during at least part of this infamous decade. Of course, all they remember are binkies and applesauce, but still ... we feel we've been given enough information to make sweeping (and probably insulting) generalizations about the people, events, and products of the entire decade.

Here's what we know: The '60s gave us baby boomers on acid, sit-ins, and the tribble-ridden Starship *Enterprise*. The decade also gave us the Berlin Wall and doomed East Germany to almost three decades of chunky, practical shoes.

Along with a fabulous multitude of consumer joys, like the cassette tape and the ingenious toy that first taught us that nothing beautiful ever lasts (the Etch A Sketch), the '60s brought with them a whole host of fashion fiascoes. While this dude-filled decade is best known for go-go boots and fringe frenzy, all the normal people were busy donning sweaters. Sweater dresses, sweater coats, sweaters that go on top of other sweaters—everybody, and we do mean *everybody*, was wearing sweaters.

As you travel through the '60s with us, you may encounter people with whom you feel you don't have much in common: a preschool Norman Bates, a foulmouthed infant, an evil villain poised to take over the world with chimpanzee-human hybrids. But just remember, each and every one of us secretly wanted to be a Beverly Hillbilly and have unlimited access to that glorious cement pond.

See? We're not so different after all.

Everybody Knows That Sherry's Loose with Her Stickers

We're pretty sure we knew this kid in elementary school. Oh, he'll tell you that if you show him yours, he'll show you his, but then he never does. He just looks at yours and then runs off. And he'll say that you're going together, but then you'll notice new Snoopy stickers on his notebook and you'll say, "Hey, where'd you get those new Snoopy stickers? Did you buy them with your allowance?" And he'll say, "No, Sherry gave them to me." And you'll say, "What the hell was that slut Sherry doing giving you stickers?" And he'll say, "Sherry's my girlfriend now." And then you'll lunge at him with your protractor and attempt to lodge it in his jugular. But you'll fail and end up with detention for an entire month, plus you'll have to talk to the school shrink once a week for the rest of the year.

It could totally happen . . . you know, hypothetically. All we're saying is: Take your hand off that zipper, honey.

Nimen Hao, Elaine! Oh, *Arigato*, Betty!

6537
MISSES' DRESS IN TWO LENGTHS
OR TUNIC, PANTS AND HAT........................ 65c
IN CANADA 75c

Extra fabric required for matching plaids, stripes, one-way design fabrics.
Use nap yardage and nap layout for satin or one-way design.
Not suitable for obvious diagonal fabrics.

Fabric required	Sizes	10	12	14	16	18	
View 1	35" or 36" without nap	3½	3¾	3¾	3¾	4½	Yds.
Dress	44" or 45"	"	3½	3¾	3¾	3¾	3¾	"
View 2	35"-36" with or without nap	3½	3¾	3¾	3¾	3¾	"
Dress	44"-45"	"	"	3½	3¾	3¾	3¾	"
View 3	35"-36" with or without nap	2½	2¾	2¾	2¾	3	"
Dress	44" or 45" without nap	1¾	1¾	2½	2¾	2¾	"
View 4	35"-36" with or without nap	1¾	1¾	2	2	2	"
Tunic	44" or 45" without nap	1¾	1¾	1¾	2	2	"
View 1, 2, 4	35"-36" with or without nap	2¾	2¾	2¾	2¾	2½	"
Pants	44" or 45" without nap	1¾	1¾	2	2¾	2½	"
Hat — 1½ yards of 35", 36" without nap, or 1 yard of 44", 45" without nap.							
Width of lower edge of dress v. 1-2		47½	48½	50½	52½	54½	Ins.
Width of lower edge of dress v. 3		42½	43½	45½	47½	49½	"
Bottom width of each pants leg v. 1, 2, 4		14¾	15	15¼	15½	15¾	"

513

Everyone in the Ladies' Auxiliary had embraced the newly popular "Far East" trend. Lacquered jewelry and cheongsam dresses were all the rage, cocktail parties often featured dim sum, and everyone on the Garden Committee went crazy over those cute little bonsai trees. But that damn Marilyn always had to take things too far.

Another Night at the Kitty Kat Crochet Club

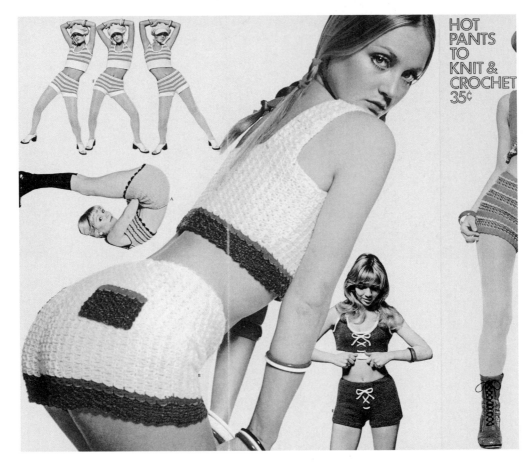

HOT
PANTS
TO
KNIT &
CROCHET
35¢

Well, to be *honest* I'm only dancing here to put myself through school. Yeah, I'm studying to be a . . . um . . . a children's speech pathologist. Yeah. I *really* want to make a difference in the world. So this is just temporary, just so I can afford school and all. Because school is *really, really* expensive.

We're *all* just doing this temporarily, actually . . . see the triplets over there? Amber, Alexa, and Ana? They're all going to be kindergarten teachers and they are *soooo smart* and *really* sweet. They don't even have boyfriends, they just come here to work and then go home and study every night.

Tiffani over there in the yellow outfit? Yeah, I guess she *is* pretty flexible. She's studying to be a paralegal. She used to work at the mall at one of those Hot Dog on a Stick places, but she just couldn't make ends meet. Her mother is *really* sick and had to have some big operation last winter, and Tiffani's just here so she can make enough to cover the medical bills. She has *such* a big heart.

Huh? The blonde over in the corner? Taking off the blue outfit? Oh God. That's Chantal. Yeah, she's just a whore. Don't even waste your time talking to her—she's not *educated* or *sophisticated* enough for a man like you.

Mmmm . . . that's right—a big smart guy like you. You're cute, you know that? I mean it! You're really cute, really smart. I think you're sweet. Now . . . about that table dance. You wanna unravel my hot pants and get things started?

Children of the Crewneck

Listen carefully, girls. For the moment, we smile. We conform to our adult oppressors' idea of adorable and we smile. But do not despair, for He Who Walks Behind the Rows has plans for us. Tonight we kill the Outlanders and gorge ourselves on Moon Pies and RC cola.

Planet of the Humanzees

Hector smiled to himself as he watched Michael take the mind-control marshmallow gently into his mouth. Michael was only the first—the first of many. Diana was coming along nicely. She had proven to be the perfect lure for unsuspecting men, men who clad themselves in curiously feminine sweaters from the Continental Hand-Knit Pattern Collection. Soon Hector would have hundreds of virile turtleneck-wearing men under his control. With these men, and his Panamanian banana connection, he would create a super race of human-chimpanzee hybrids. Then no one could stop him. Hector and his humanzees would rule the world! MWAAAA HAAAA HAAA HAAA HA!

Ginger Is Madder Than a Skipper with No Dinner

Ginger always knew that the Professor was a whiz with coconut radios and stationary-bike power generators, but she never dreamed that he'd actually pull off the S.S. *Minnow* Makeover-O-Matic. Mary Ann had gone in looking like a 15-year-old bumpkin and had come out blond! Blond and tall! Blond and tall . . . *with Ginger's signature loopy swoopy hairdo.* And to top it all off, this new and improved Mary Ann had even managed to master the one-knee-bent movie star stance. This wouldn't do, wouldn't do at all. Ginger had to disable the machine before that uppity bitch Mrs. Howell got a turn. This would most certainly call for an elaborate plan involving headhunter costumes and Gilligan in a dress.

Look! I Made My Little Sister Disappear!

50 CENTS

Book No. 109

PATONS

Family Speedknits
by *Beehive*

Now all I have to do is tell you what I saw Daddy doing to that woman when I came home early from my friend's house that Saturday you were at Grandma's and . . . POOF! Your marriage is over too! TAAAAAAAAAAADAAAAAAAAAAA!

TRADE WIND
MODEL No. 2012

TRADE WIND

MODEL No. 2012

Sizes: 12, 14 and 16 (Sizes 14 and 16 in parenthesis)

Materials: Pauline Denham SIERRA, 2 (3-3) sks Color A, 2 sks each of Colors B and C; Nos. 2 and 3 straight needles (or whatever size necessary to maintain st gauge).

Gauge: 8 sts = 1"

Back: With No. 2 needles and Color A, cast on 137 (145-153) sts. Work seed st: **Row 1:** K 1, p 1 and repeat, end k 1. **Row 2:** Same as Row 1. Work 12 rows. Change to No. 3 needles and stockinette st (k 1 row, p 1 row). Work in stripes as follows: Tie in Color B, work 6 rows. With Color C, work 4 rows. With Color A, work as follows: **Row 1:** * K 1, sl next st as if to p, repeat from * across row, end k 1. **Row 2:** P. With Color B, work 6 rows. With Color C, work 4 rows. With Color A, work 4 rows. Repeat these 6 stripes consecutively for entire sweater. Work even until piece measures 11". **Shape Armholes:** Cast off 8 (9-10) sts once each end, then dec 1 st each end every other row 6 times = 109 (115-121) sts. Work until armhole measures 5½ (6-6½)" straight from start of shaping, **Shape Neck and Shoulders:** Work across 34 (36-38) sts. Cast off next 41 (43-45) sts. Finish row. Work the 2 sides separately. Dec at neck edge, 3 sts 2 times and 2 sts 3 times = 22 (24-26) sts. Cast off. Tie in color necessary to keep stripes even and work other shoulder to correspond.

Front: Work same as back.

Finishing: Bias Bands: With No. 3 needles and Color A, cast on 9 sts. **Row 1:** P. **Row 2:** K 2 tog, k 6, inc in last st. Repeat these 2 rows. Make bands long enough to go across front and back necklines and around each armhole. Block all pieces. Sl st shoulder and side seams. Sew bias binding around neck edge and armholes.

TRADE WIND
MODEL No. 2012

Wow. How many chili dogs and orders of red beans and rice do you think your diet has to contain to earn you the nickname "Trade Wind"? Classy, my dear, very classy.

UGH. I hope that noise was a foghorn.

Lanyards of Lust

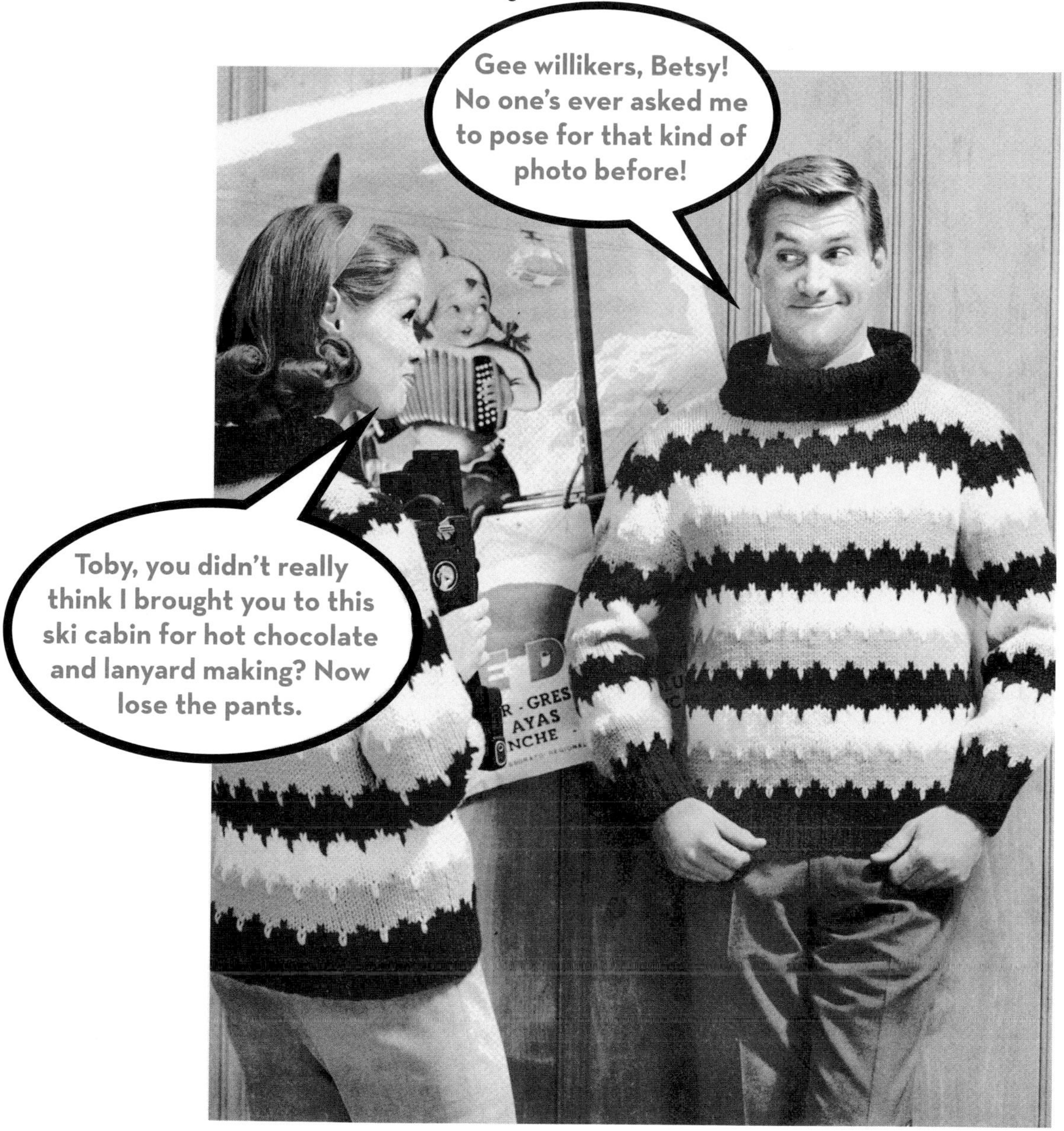

Frankfurter-Fingered Friends Forever

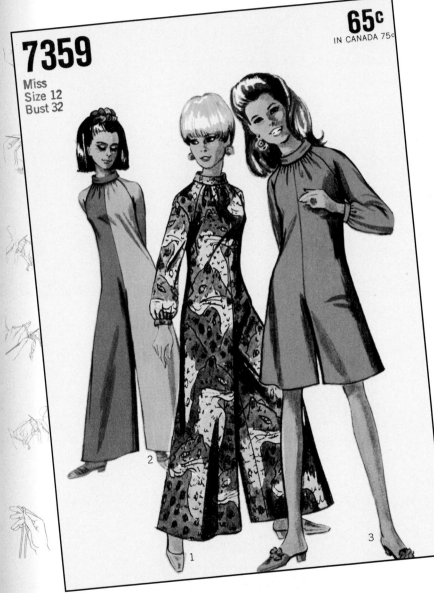

7359

Miss
Size 12
Bust 32

65¢
IN CANADA 75¢

Years later, medical science would discover that the Potted Possum Parts so often ingested during college hazing rituals could cause Giganticheaditis, the inability to look straight ahead, a strange attraction to culotte onesies, and the rare condition known as hot dog fingers.

But the girls of Delta Zeta already knew all that. They found out the hard way.

Love Thy Parents

In the Wild

The Elusive Knit-Bodied Peafowl have been kept and reared in captivity for more than 2,000 years. Although some signs of domestication have occurred, such as the ability to walk upright, apply lip gloss, and read tabloid magazines, no changes in shape or size are present.

Knit-Bodied Peafowl are famous not only for their beautiful appearance, but also for their peculiar behavior. This particular breed of peafowl is notorious for being rather quarrelsome, often demonstrating their displeasure by urinating on innocent bystanders. They do no get along with other domestic animals, perhaps considering themselves to be unique creatures, which they undoubtedly are.

The long ornamental feathers, which the Knit-Bodied Peafowl displays so magnificently here, are part of an elaborate courtship display. During the mating season, the feathers elevate to form a massive, lacy fan, supported from behind by the unadorned tail feathers. This sight is accompanied by rasping noises from the fluttered wings, prancing movements of the feet, and repeated cries of *"I'm sooooo drunk. Oh God, I'm sooooo drunk."*

The act of copulation is surprisingly brief, and afterward the Knit-Bodied Peafowl tends to become angry and snappish. The male Peafowl wisely keeps his distance until a new mating season begins, while the female knits a warm nest for roosting. In three weeks' time, the Knit-Bodied Peafowl will lay three to five brownish buff eggs. The beauty of life begins anew.

Play Your Hand, Stan. Play Your Hand.

Aran Knitting in Double Double
see page 4

Hey, whatcha got in your pocket there, Stan? You're kinda making me nervous . . . the way you never take your hand out of there.

You've got to be freakin' kidding me, Stan. Not this again. *Show me your hand.*
I said show it to me, dammit.

What? I *know* there's a child here. But I ask you, Stan: Who's the one being childish? You, Stan. It's you. Now, just stop being an ass and show me what's in your hand.

Matching Pullovers
see page 15

Look, the kid is even offering you her ice cream cone if you will just show us what is in your freaking hand.

What's that? You're ready to show us? It's about time. I've been worrying myself to death thinking about all of the horrible things it could be.

Let's see . . . What? . . . Is that a human tooth? And what's that other thing? A thumb bone? A metacarpal, you say?

Oh. Carry on, then. Sorry to have bothered you, Stan.

Just Nubbins Now

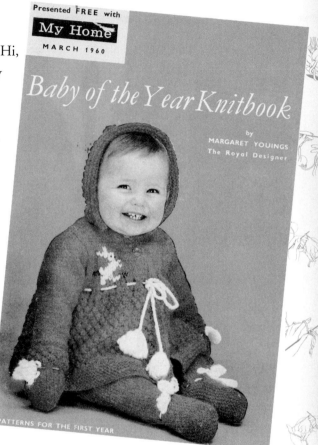

Presented FREE with
My Home
MARCH 1960

Baby of the Year Knitbook

by
MARGARET YOUINGS
The Royal Designer

PATTERNS FOR THE FIRST YEAR

Excuse me, ma'am—sir. Excuse me. Yes, you. Hi. Hi, there. I was wondering . . . You see, I think I may be in a bit of a jam here. It's just that . . . well, I can't seem to feel my fingers. Or my toes. Hell, I can't even bend my knees. It also seems that I can't turn my head at all. The hairy-chested man with the camera who keeps chatting up my mom says to keep smiling, and I'm doing the best I can, but frankly I'm a little concerned. Since I can't look down, I was wondering if you could tell me: Do I still *have* fingers and toes? I mean, are they just numb or are they actually *missing*?

What? What was that? *I look like an idiot in this stupid red suit?* Is that what you said? Look, asshole, I didn't *ask* you for your opinion. I simply asked you to verify the existence of my appendages. Why do you have to get all snarky? It's not like I *chose* this outfit, you moron. A kid's gotta make a living. My mom's in between meal tickets right now, and ever since that f——ing babyface Artie stole the Gerber campaign, I've had to lower my standards a bit. Besides, can't you read? I am "Baby of the Year." Baby of the *Year,* man. Don't you get that?

What? I look like a what? *A giant inflamed whitehead?* Look, jackass, as soon as I find my hands I'm gonna show you *exactly* which finger is my favorite.

America's Next Top Mannequin

Since the "Learn to Be a Model" course was full (and way out of their price range), Lucy, Beth, and Charlotte had to settle for the "Learn to Be a Mannequin" class. It wasn't nearly as glamorous as they had hoped. Plus, after a while their backs got to hurting. And the pigeons! Lucy had to get five stitches when one of the little buggers mistook her edgy head wrap for a bolt of cotton candy. Still, in order to be true to their craft they had to remain absolutely still. (Blinking was allowed, though not encouraged.)

Three Rules for Good Livin'

OK, so at first glance we thought these very '60s dresses were kinda cute. We were even down with the headband and flippy 'do. But then we realized that these mod getups violate one of Mary and Kimberly's Three Rules of Good Living. For your own personal edification, we provide all three rules here:

1. **Never wear an outfit that comes with its own belt (see photograph).**

2. **Never eat at a restaurant if "Restaurant" is the biggest word on the sign.**

3. **Never trust a naked bus driver.**

Ah, the Good Mole Days

"I'm really glad you could make it to the reunion, Debbie. I can't believe it's been 20 years since we were high school sweethearts. And here we are both single again. We had some good times, didn't we? Say, do you still have that little mole on your you-know-what that used to drive me wild?"

"I sure do, honey. In fact, I've grown moles all over my body. I had this one mole that popped up on my chin a few years ago. It had this gray hair that grew out of it, and I kept having to remember to pluck it out. Sometimes I would forget and my kid would say, 'Ewww, Mommy. You're gross.' Anyway, it started to turn purple around the edges—the mole, not the hair—and my doctor said we'd better cut it off and make sure I didn't have the cancer. It hurt like the dickens when he cut that thing off, and I had to wear a Band-Aid on my chin for weeks. Well, it turns out that I didn't have the cancer after all, which was a *huge* relief, especially since I'd just gone through that whole ordeal with the hemorrhoids. . . .

"Hey, Sugar, where are you going?"

95 CENTS

PATONS
Book No. 105

Astra Easy-Knits for the Family
by *Beehive*

O h, Father, you are a charming bloke. It's too bad that you will have to be eliminated. You see, it's the only way that I can have Mother all to myself, and I must have her. Yes, I must. So you will "fall" down a well shaft and I will be Mother forever . . . oh, I mean be *with* Mother forever. With.

When I Think About You,
I Touch My Shell

LORELEI
MODEL No. 2002

H ere we see Lorelei discovering that rolling around sexily on the beach just isn't the same alone. All the panty sand, none of the payoff.

Cookie Combat

"Look, you heard the photographer. Just eat your damn cookie."

"You eat *your* cookie! I don't even know where these things came from. Besides, I know what you're trying to pull."

"What are you talking about? He said eat the cookie. Now, *eat it.*"

"It's bad enough that you got to the photo shoot first and took the blue sweater. I look like a complete idiot because my sweater exactly matches my hair. Now you're trying to fatten me up, too?"

"Fatten you up? Me? I believe somebody beat me to the punch on that one. And it's not my fault you dyed your hair the color of orange sherbet."

"You are such a total bitch. Everyone hates you."

"Everyone except your boyfriend."

"Oh, I will *so* cut you."

"Bring it on, carrottop. Bring it on."

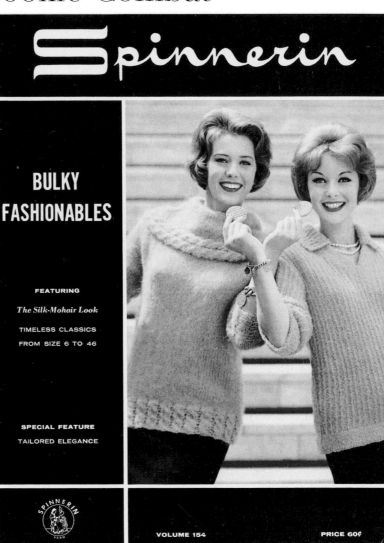

Socialite Spite

Midge didn't care how nice they pretended to be. She knew those Junior League bitches had been jealous ever since her mad-scientist husband gave her Mini-Midge for Christmas.

THE '70s

Smurfs on Acid and Fancy Manotards

Ah, the '70s. The decade that brought us beauty, wit, talent, grace, and unsurpassable good taste. But enough about the births of Mary and Kimberly.

The '70s also brought us many other wonderful things, including the Village People, *The Brady Bunch*, and the unforgettable *Shaft*. This groovy decade also gave us an excuse to say things like "But, Paw, I can fish as good as any boy" and "The plane! The plane!"

But what about the clothes? At first glance, you may think that mocking '70s-ish ideas of what was stylin' would be difficult, given the fact that these days we all prance around in low-slung, flared jeans and knee-high leather high-heeled boots. But let us remind you that the retro fashions of today are merely *inspired* by the '70s. That's inspired by, not copied from. The actual '70s contained fashion atrocities the likes of which the modern world has not seen before or since. And sadly, these clothing catastrophes were not confined to retail products. People made plenty of homemade ugly, too. They crocheted full-body manotards for their children. They covered themselves in handcrafted coats so enormous, hairy, and out of control that they took on the appearance of giant freebasing Smurfs. The swinging '70s also gave us fashion's immortal archnemesis: the poncho. Oh, poncho, how you mock us. When will it end? It's been 30 years. *Why won't you die?*

The Swinging '70s

jiffy
easy cut · easy sew

5 main pattern pieces each

5685
SIMPLE-TO-SEW — MEN'S OR MISSES'
JIFFY® KIMONO ROBE IN TWO LENGTHS $1.00
IN S. A. & CANADA 1.10
NOTE: THIS ENVELOPE CONTAINS ONLY ONE PATTERN . . . EITHER THE MEN'S KIMONO ROBE OR
THE MISSES' KIMONO ROBE.

What do you mean you're uncomfortable? It's just Susan and Tom. They're our *friends,* and they invited us over for dinner. Try to be polite. Look how excited they are to have us here.

What? I *told* you already. They thought it would be fun if we all wore our robes. Like a pajama party. They thought it would help us all loosen up a bit . . . you know, have a good time. They throw these parties all the time. They're supposed to be a real blast. I heard Susan is the best hostess in town.

Why aren't they wearing pajamas under their robes? How should I know? What are you so worried about? Oh, and Tom says that we're having dinner in the bedroom so that we can eat while we recline like the ancient Romans did. Sounds fun, huh?

Tom? *Looking* at you? What do you mean *looking* at you? Listen, honey, everything's fine. What you need is to have a few drinks and relax. It's gonna be a great evening. Oh, and they mentioned something about swing dancing after dinner. I didn't know they were into that, but boy, I haven't done the Lindy Hop in ages!

A Triumph for *Lonnie*'s Fantasy, Anyway

20
A mini-bolero: its somewhat bizarre design will off-set the classic lines of a plain roll-neck sweater.

A TRIUMPH FOR FANTASY...

Yo, my name is Lonnie. Yeah, I work at this stupid crochet magazine. I know, it's lame, but after my mom kicked me out I really needed some cash. Anyway, I call this a Crobra. Not to be confused with either a cobra or a crowbar. Crochet + bra, get it? They wouldn't let me put the name in the magazine, but anyway, that's what it's called. It's for chicks, but I really designed it with us guys in mind. See, the bra is on *top* of the shirt. That means it's easier to get off because you can see it better. No more fumbling under the sweater. And here's the really genius part: It has just a tie in the front and that's it. None of those brackety things that only Fonzie can get undone. But the best part? There are targets on the boobs! How kick-ass is that? I figure, men like targets and men like boobs—why not put the two together? Plus, it makes for really good date jokes . . . like "I have you in my sights now" or "That outfit is right on target," or you can just poke 'em and yell "BULL'S-EYE!" You can't buy lines that smooth!

You're welcome, dudes, you're welcome.

Lord of the Dance

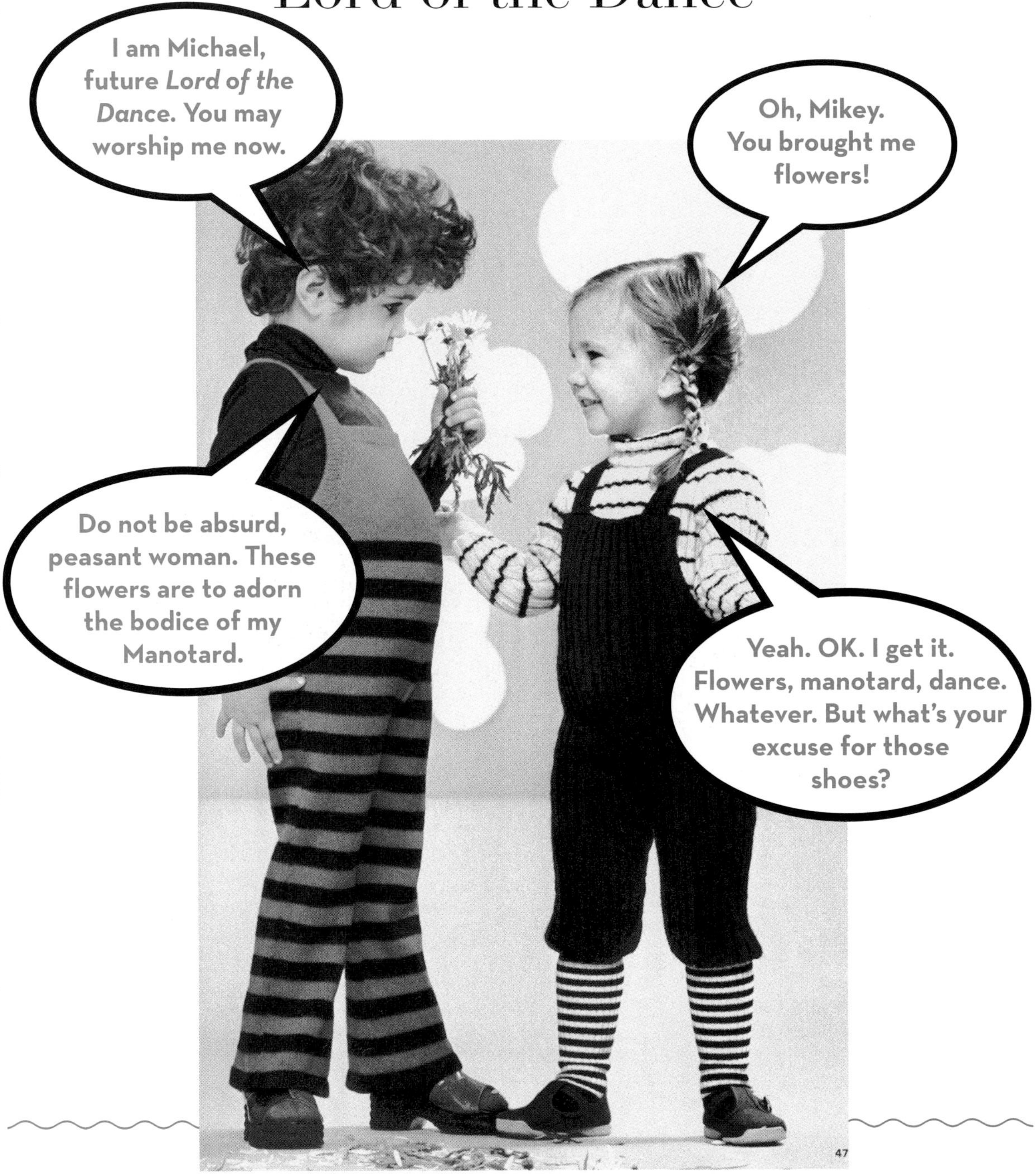

And Now . . . a Little Posing
for *the Ladies*

Despite his happy marriage to Barbara and successful career as a CPA, Rodger feels unfulfilled.

Oh sure, sure . . . he knows he's not the best-looking guy. But Rodger feels he has a certain something, a raw sexual magnetism that could have been properly exploited if he had only had the opportunity to pursue his dream career. For Rodger knows, deep down inside, that he *should have been a model for the JCPenney catalog.*

He also knows that this dream can never be realized—the twins have just started orthodontic treatment and the house needs to be recarpeted. Barbara would never understand. But sometimes, at night when she's gone to her weekly mah-jongg game, Rodger locks the door to the bedroom and indulges in a little fantasy modeling session.

Awww yeah.

4538

Emu
Betty
Horwood

DK
DOUBLE
KNITTING

4
PLY

38-50 inch

SEVEN SIZES

the wool Bin
451 lakeshore road east, oakville, ontario, canada
telephone 845-9512

7$\frac{1}{2}$p

The Story of One Family
(with Lots of Matching Sweaters)

Leaflet 1042 / 50¢

Lady Galt®

Wrap Sweaters

Instructions for adults and children using Lady Galt machine launderable double knitting/knitting worsted sayelle* or bulky sayelle*

Traduction française des abréviations incluses

This family seems very happy together. Daddy and Timmy like to dress in matching sweaters. Sometimes Mommy also joins in the fun. They go to the park together, to the movies, and even to the market. They even have fun together while shopping for produce!

"Say, honey, that's a mighty big melon. It sure is a handful! Don't you think you should get two melons? It only seems right for you to have two melons. I'll even hold them for you. You want me to hold your melons?"

"Oh, Tom. You're so bad. Not in front of Timmy."

"Hoho! Only joking, only joking. Right, Timmy?"

"Right, Daddy. Oh, Daddy, you are funny. I'm funny like you. Wanna hear a joke?"

"Sure, Timmy"

"Knock. Knock."

"Who's there?"

"Olive."

"Olive who?"

"Olive you, Daddy."

"And I love you, Timmy."

In the photo:

In this next photo, we can see that things have changed a bit for the family. While Timmy is at his ancient Aunt Helen's house, Daddy confronts Mommy about the affair she's been having for the last six years with their produce guy, Carl. Mommy says that she doesn't love Carl, but that Carl really knows his way around a pair of melons. This makes Daddy angry, and Daddy threatens Mommy. Mommy giggles, because that is what Mommy does when Mommy is uncomfortable.

Leaflet 1045 / 50c

Lady Galt

Wrap Coats

Instructions for adults and children
using Lady Galt machine launderable
double knitting/knitting worsted sayelle*
or bulky sayelle*
Traduction française des abréviations incluses

For the first time, it occurs to Daddy that Timmy might not be his son. Daddy has always been fond of Timmy, but to be honest, Daddy doesn't want to work his fingers to the bone to put sloppy joes on the table for Carl's kid. Mommy is shocked. (That is her shocked face that you see in this photo. Mommy is not a very good emoter.)

Timmy is worried, but secretly curious. He wonders if Carl would give him free apples if he asked.

Leaflet 1043 / 50c

Lady Galt. Cardigans

Instructions for adults and children, using Lady Galt machine launderable double knitting/knitting worsted sayelle* or bulky sayelle*
Traduction française des abréviations incluses

This is Mommy and Timmy at a mall four hours from their house. Mommy is telling Timmy that she is going to go away and that Timmy must stay here at the mall. Mommy says that someone nice will come along and take Timmy home with them. She is just sure of it! Mommy has put a barrette in Timmy's hair to disguise him. She tells him that if anyone asks, his name is Tammy and that his mommy and daddy were killed by Canadian terrorists.

What Timmy doesn't know is that Daddy has said, "You can have me or Timmy and the melons. You choose." And Mommy has chosen Daddy, because melons aren't that important to her anyway. She prefers bananas.

Jerkin My Tudor

When you first look at the cover of this knitting pattern book, you might find yourself drawn to the woman with the oversized and oddly placed nipple. That, along with the kangaroo pouch hanging off her abdomen, would seem to be entertainment enough. But I suggest that we take a closer look at the pink-clad Casanova at the bottom right.

I don't know if it's the squinty eyes, the butterscotch comb-over, the manboobs, or his pre–*Queer Eye* knack for putting together a look that pops, but this Tudor Jerkin guy is H-O-T. That handlebar mustache isn't hurting anything either. Or his resemblance to the totally rad (and unfortunately deceased) Captain Kangaroo. And what woman doesn't love a man who sees the world through amber-colored glasses? Don't you just want to rip off this stud's belted, horizontal-ribbed sweater, red tie, pink textured striped button-down, and red lacy corset? What? You don't think he's wearing a corset? Take it from someone who knows: You don't get cleavage like that without some support.

Hot for Horsey

So anyway, then Connie says, "You can't love Topper. He's a horse." And I was like, "Why are you always bringing that up? What does that have to do with anything?" And she was all "You need a boyfriend. Like a real boyfriend." And I told her that you *are* my real boyfriend. And she said that you couldn't be my real boyfriend because we couldn't even be together . . . you know, like *be* together. And then I showed her that catalog with the harnesses and stuff and—well, that just shut her right up.

So anyway, what time are you picking me up for Winter Formal?

That, or I Roll You Down the Stairs on the Damn Thing

O K, this is the last time I'm going to ask. Get off of the rolly horse and give me my turn or I am going to take this foot—yes, this adorable stripy foot right here—unbutton your fanny flap, and ram my toasty little tootsies right up that selfish, spoiled little ass of yours.

And He's Ribbed for Her Pleasure

"Yeah, so I went to my friend Stephan and I told him that I wanted a marcasite ring that was the exact color of a cheesy, early-'70s porn-star mustache. I can't believe he got it exactly right!"

"Well, you know, lady . . . I have other hair that color, too."

♪ *Bomp chicha bow now* ♪

"Hey, where's that music coming from?"

Every 28 Days Suzanne Seriously Considers Running Away

It was hard being the only Nelson triplet with arms. It's not that Suzanne wasn't grateful to have all four limbs. She was. After all, she could actually style her hair, unlike Becky, whose hair lay limp, and Maggie, who had given up and shaved hers. It was just that the other girls teased her, calling her Army McElbows and making fun of her complicated sweaters with sleeves. Plus, the boys seemed to prefer her nubby sisters. They were more fun. They drank beer straight from the tap, they never had to be the designated driver, and they loved to make out with the fellas—rolling around and around and around and around . . .

But by far the worst part of being the only armed Nelson triplet was that she was forever in charge of all potty issues. Nothing kills the mood on a date like your sister desperately calling your name from the restaurant bathroom: "Suuu-zaaa-aaaanne. Wiiiiipies!"

The Many Moods of a Pattern Model

SHY

ASS-KISSY

ANNOYINGLY CHIPPER

NOT STONED ENOUGH

GASSY

HOLY CRAP! I MODEL CROCHET BERETS FOR A LIVING. HOW THE HELL DID THIS HAPPEN?

They Wouldn't Let Poor Rudolph Join in Any Reindeer Games

Growing up at the North Pole wasn't all that bad. It did suck to never be allowed outside, but after all, everything was completely covered in ice and snow, so why would you want to? And Santa had done his very best in the "season rooms" to approximate fall, spring, and summer so that the little elflets would know what a complete year looked like in the rest of the world.

But some things were bad. Like having to make your own damn Christmas toys, and having to learn about the birds and the birds by watching Prancer and Dancer constantly humping each other.

Also, You Might Try a Little Zoloft.
That Usually Helps.

Now we'd like to take a moment to open the Threadbared mailbag:

Dear Dr. Kimberly and Dr. Mary,

I have a dilemma. I long to make beautiful matching sweaters for my entire family. I hunger for the embarrassment of coordinating cardigans and compatible crewnecks. I want to watch gleefully as my husband and children try to hide in shame from people they know at Stuckey's. There's only one problem: In order to know what kind of matchy matchy mayhem to unleash on my family, I have to figure out what kind of sweaters to make. I'm stumped. I was hoping you could offer some expert advice.

Sincerely,
Matchy McTackypants

Dear Matchy,

What a great question! We're so glad you asked. There are, in fact, several easily defined types of families in the world, and knowing which kind of sweater to make is simply a matter of discovering which type of family you are. We just happen to have the list of family types right here in our Big Book of Psychobabble. It's as simple as reading the descriptions and looking at the pictures to identify what type of family you have. Here are the three types.

The Mountain Climbing Family

THE MOUNTAIN CLIMBING FAMILY

For those who attempt mountain climbing, here are carefree, comfortable, warm cabled pullovers.

15 to 17 - Three identical tubular pullovers knitted in wide cables and ribbing. Straight neck edge. Knitting Worsted Weight.

The Tennis Family

TENNIS FASHION FOR EVERYONE

This cardigan of a classic shape but with an unusual touch will be unanimously chosen by the whole family.

22 to 24 - A bicolor stripe accents the neckline, the fastening band and the wrists of this long cardigan knitted in stockinette stitch and accented by groups of thin cables. Sport Weight Yarn.

And finally, the Sea Dog Family

THE "SEA DOG" FAMILY

For those who like the outdoors and sailboats, here are the bulky Breton sailor pullovers with their matching striped cap.

to 14 - Three identical ...ilor pullovers knitted in ...tockinette stitch, with a ...olid color yoke over a ...riped background, sewn-in ...eeves, squared neck edge, ...oupled with a ribbed cap. ...ort Weight Yarn.

That's it. Mountain climbers, tennis players, or sea dogs. Once you identify your familial type, you should be well on your way to making shameful sweaters for the whole fam! Hope this helps.

Dr. Kimberly and Dr. Mary

UPDATE

Dear Dr. Kimberly and Dr. Mary,

I'm confused. My family doesn't seem to fit any of the types. We've never been mountain climbing—my son Naven has a fear of thermoses. We aren't interested in tennis and I don't think we want to be any kind of "dogs." Please help. What should we do?

Sincerely,
Matchy McTackypants

Dear Matchy,

Wow. This is awkward. We're not sure how to tell you this. If you don't fit one of the types, then, well . . . you're . . . how do we say this? You're not a *family*. We're sorry to have to be the ones to tell you. You'll have to begin to distance yourselves from one another. You really shouldn't even be living together. Wow. This is such a shame. Oh, and you should probably seek some help to deal with the loss of your "awkward grouping of people who have no hobbies but thought that they were kin"—like counseling or something, but we don't do that. So good luck!

Dr. Kimberly and Dr. Mary

The Sisterhood

"So I've been working on this really groovy song for the Friendship Circle Ceremony this Friday. I just hope Reverend Goddess Moonfire will let me play it. My heart tells me that it will inspire and uplift the entire Sisterhood. I call it 'My Holy Uterus.' It's all about the beauty and miracle of a woman's body and how we should remain pure and untainted by the filth of man. And how women should come together and flourish in the bonds of sisterhood, supporting and nurturing one another and sharing our innermost hopes, dreams, and true selves, thus transcending this earthly realm. It supports all of the teachings of the Sisterhood, and I think that it will really help us bask in the pure light of our womanhood. As soon as we get back from this patchouli run, I'm going to play my song for Reverend Goddess Moonfire. That's exactly what I'll do. Hey, Bettina, are you listening?"

"What? Oh yeah. Whatever, Juniper. Hey, do you see that guy over there on the motorcycle? He is totally hot! Woooooooooweeeeeee! Maybe if I hold my leg like this he can see the pure light of my womanhood through this skirt."

Adoption Is the New Black

"Look, lady, I told you, I don't *need* to be adopted. My parents are right over there at the King Tut Hut buying Cleopatra key chains and tiny souvenir spoons. I'm sure you're a really nice lady and I appreciate the dress, even if it is a little on the whorish side. But this hat—what is this? A turban? I told you, I'm from *Chicago*. I'm *Presbyterian*. Now, let go of my hand and give me back my Princess Jasmine underpants."

Love Guppy in a Poncho. Wasn't That a Van Gogh Painting?

hats and scarves by *Lady Galt*

Hats, scarves, mitts and a muff, to knit or crochet in new Lady Galt Fairy Floss hand knitting yarn. A soft, luxurious blend of mohair and orlon.

Leaflet 1031 - .50¢

It would appear that Lady Galt has a thing for these mysterious black-clad creatures. They are exactly what I would imagine the result would be if Disney created a sex-education video and used costumed humans to portray Mickey's sperm. For this reason, we'll call them Spickies. Anyway, it seems these Spickies are quite adventurous little buggers. They like to frolic about the countryside sporting colorful hats and scarves.

Spickies also occasionally venture out into the world in ponchos so colorful and happy that they make me want to go outside, jump in my car, and cut someone off in traffic, just to balance out the universe.

Now, I'm no biologist, but in terms of who's gonna reach the egg, my money's on the Spickie in the hooded thing with the thunder thighs. Those thighs say "good swimmer."

capes and things by *Lady Galt*

Fun Ideas in fashionable cover-ups to knit or crochet. Featuring new Lady Galt Fairy Floss hand knitting yarn. A soft, luxurious blend of mohair and orlon.
Leaflet 1032 - .50¢

And don't you go thinking that Spickies are only for grown-ups. After all, what better way to introduce your kids to the facts of life than by giving them a gigantic stuffed Spickie to play with? Now, doesn't she look superexcited? Hanging out with your Spickie while you ride a giant chicken. What fun!

Hats, scarves, and ponchos for stuffed Spickie are sold separately. Also, coming this fall, the Spickie Dream House!

Smaller Than an Anorexic June Bug

We've heard of sweaters designed to make your breasts look larger. And we've seen sweaters that draw attention to your breasts—mostly on network television, sure, but we still feel secure in the knowledge that they exist. This sweater, however, baffles us. It seems to say, "Hey, buddy, you're going to need glasses to see these peaches. Seriously, these things are smaller than preemie Smurfs. And my nips? Oh, they'll just appear as tiny minute dots, about the size of a grit." (That's the singular form of grits, for you Northerners.) Also, the sweater seems to imply that one's breasts are shaped like crudely drawn flowers. Huh.

She Also Plays the Harpsichord!

G600
75¢

LADIES'
PANTY
GIRDLE

PATTERN
INCLUDES
SIZES S, M, L, XL

Sew Lovely

LINGERIE PATTERN BY LAVERNE DEVEREAUX

LAYOUT AND SEWING INSTRUCTIONS INCLUDED

Oh, she is *sexy*. Look at the sexually elusive "more is more" approach to the pattern at left. After all, what good is a pair of panties if they don't completely obscure your belly button?

And be honest. Is there *anything* sexier than a woman who sews her own lingerie? I can hear the guys now: "Seriously, Tom, you should totally go out with Sandra. She has a great personality *and* she makes her own panties."

That's hot.

Daddy's Double-Barrel Discipline

the beehive **aran look**   95 cents   **PATONS**

It seemed harsh, but Augustus knew that a leg full of lead would teach little Emily that it was wrong to go around mercilessly stretching the tongues of her pets.

When Wool Becomes Fur!

WHEN WOOL BECOMES FUR

Fur stitch is having a fantastic success. Models made in this stitch are reminiscent of the traditional coats of Greek and Afghan shepherds, which the present day taste for exotic clothes has brought back into fashion.

You loved *When Animals Attack!* You couldn't get enough of *When Men Become Women!* You were glued to your sets for *When Syphilis Spreads!*

Now, coming this fall from Thread-bared TV . . . *WHEN WOOL BE-COMES FUR!*

You'll watch as unsuspecting crafters fashion themselves full-body wool coverings!

You'll gaze in wonder as they choose bizarre and unflattering color combinations!

You'll gasp in horror as the awkwardly hued wool slowly but surely . . . *becomes fur!*

You'll marvel at how it attaches itself to their skin!

You'll weep as you hear their heartbreaking stories!

You may never knit again!

Also! A rare bonus feature, chock-full of emotional turmoil: *FURRY CRAFTERS AND THE FAMILIES WHO LOVE THEM!*

You'll watch as families cope with this hairy situation.

You'll be touched as they don hideous vests to make their loved one feel accepted.

You'll sob as you realize that your family would never make that kind of sacrifice for you.

Tune in Tuesday at 4:30 A.M. on Threadbared TV.

THE '80s

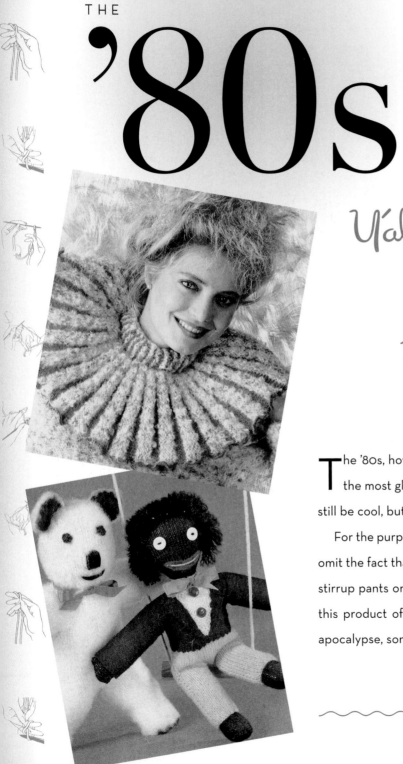

U'all Come Back Now, Ya Hear?

The '80s, how we love thee. You are currently stuck in the most glorious place in fashion history: too old to still be cool, but not old enough to be vintage and classy.

For the purposes of this discussion, we will conveniently omit the fact that a certain large retail chain was still selling stirrup pants on its site in 2006. (Though, considering that this product offering is most surely a sign of the coming apocalypse, someone should look into it.)

Anyway, the Jovi Chick bangs, the pleated pants, the leg warmers . . . the '80s are ripe with mocking potential. But we here at Threadbared would hate to take the easy road. So instead of taking obvious shots at girls wearing shoulder pads who fold over their jeans and then roll them up, we'll take a stroll with racist toddlers and attend church with Sister Man Hands and her crocheted Bible covers.

And we'll take you on a little trip down our way. Come on down south, y'all, and meet your inbred redneck cousins. They got crocheted britches, and darn if they don't just beat all!

Oh, '80s, we know we'll see you again. You'll be back just like every other decade before you. We'll be here, waiting, and keeping our Jellies warm just in case.

Sweaters of the Damned

Hayfield

THERMAL

1775
30–46

Chunky

Awwww . . . look at the happy couple in the matching sweaters! So cute, so sweet, so carefree . . . and wait, *are they also wearing matching corduroy pants*? Yes! *Yes, they are!* Are they not the perfect picture of adorableness?

But wait . . . what . . . what *in the hell* is going on in the background? Is it the apocalypse? The Second Coming? Is that a cold wind blowing their hair back? Are the terrified screams of lost souls swirling all around them?

Any minute now, they're going to turn around and realize what's happening.

"Wha . . . huh . . . what the? AAAAGGGGHHH! Forget the chunky thermal sweaters . . . it's the *rapture*! For f——'s sake, put that camera down! *Run for your lives!*"

Don't Ask How Carl Goes Potty. Just . . . Don't.

Oh sure, having conjoined-twin myslexia was sometimes fun. 'Cause, like, almost no one else had it, so it kinda made Timmy special. Plus, he always had a buddy around to play with. And Timmy really did love his twin, Carl.

But it sucks when your conjoined twin is so much better at everything. Carl was better at baseball, growing mustaches, playing Barbies . . . everything. But what really burned Timmy up was when Carl was named the team MVP and wouldn't even let Timmy hold the trophy. After all, it was *Timmy's* legs that had run all those bases. (Carl's legs had flailed around as they neared home, but everyone knew it was just a useless reflex.)

Buzz Cut Barbie

We totally recognize the chick on the left. She's that Barbie that your cousin's friend cuts all the hair off of because she has like eight Barbies and only one Ken. So she shears the most mannish Barbie she has and goes about her Barbie Dream House business. But you, being a very literal and sensitive little kid, can't accept a Ken without a fully intact man lump where his penis should be.

Big Hands, I Know You're the One

We offer this up as proof that no one gets everything they pray for, not even good people who dress conservatively, attend church, play the guitar at prayer meeting, and make special home-made handicrafts, including custom Bible covers to gently cradle the word of the Lord.

Because if they did, how would you explain the truck driver face, shoe salesman comb-over, and big ol' strapping man hands on that church lady?

Social Progress

Behold the Golliwog in all his glory:

We believe this pattern is from sometime in the '60s. We were shocked by how freakishly scary it is. What the hell kinda kid would want to play with this thing? Check out those crazy eyes. And it's also a tad offensive. Wow. Have some stereotypes with your milk and cookies, kids. Thank goodness by the time we were growing up in the '80s, our culture had moved past such horrible displays of racial intolerance and misunderstanding.

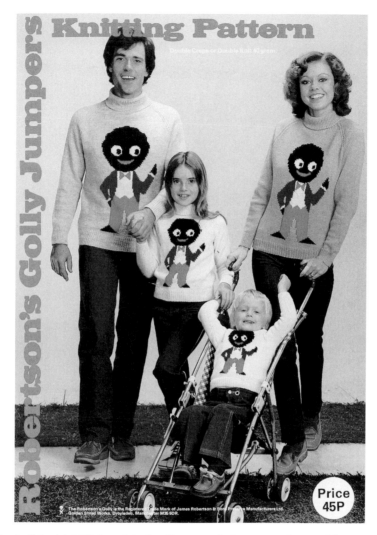

Or not. What the hell is this? Either this family is on their way to the weekly meeting of the Racist Memorabilia Collectors Club (Cracker Division), or they're just cruising to get their asses kicked down at the Family Dollar. Either way, they are totally psyched about it. Check out that kid in the stroller. "We hate black people! Up with whitey! Wheeeeee!"

Ten bucks says they have a Mammy cookie jar on their kitchen counter and a lawn jockey out by the carport.

Grocery Store Feet*
(or Trailer Toes, If You Prefer)

After a delightful afternoon digging up cat turds in the old sandpile, Travis and his cousins Mindy Sue and Jo Beth geared up for a trip to the swimming hole.

Things hadn't been the same at the old hole since they lost Granny in that turkey-frying accident. Granny made their extra-special crocheted swimming britches. She used to take them to the hole all the time, and she would bring along pork skins and Tang for the kids to snack on. Without her, they were forced to resort to obtaining their own afternoon goodies. Today that wasn't a problem, on account of Travis had filled his bucket nearly full at the sandpile.

Now they had to go with creepy Uncle Clint, but he said if they behaved, he might take them down to the Piggly Wiggly to ride the mechanical chicken out front. So they had that at least. Besides, Travis was always tickled to have his two favorite cousins to play with. Years later, he would refer to them as "common law wife #1" and "that bitch that stole my truck and a whole freezer full of doe meat."

*A helpful definition from the *Threadbared* dictionary, for our Yankee readers. *Grocery store feet* (n): When the soles of your feet turn a yucky black color from walking barefoot in the Piggly Wiggly (acceptable substitutes include the Winn-Dixie and the Kroger).

Eat Your Heart Out, Preppie

Behold this young woman's unruly curls, the way she tucks in bulky sweaters, and her ability to be both fun-loving and deadly serious. Also notice her thick, overgrown eyebrows, her fondness for pleated pants, and her ambiguously Hispanic/Italian/Whatever appearance. There can be only one explanation for all of these magical traits emerging in the same individual. That's right, you guessed it—we have uncovered the long-lost secret love child of Jessie Spano and A. C. Slater. Oh sure, Jessie would have had to give birth sometime around the time that Zack was charming the skirt off Miss Bliss, but I think the resemblance is undeniable. Now we know why Slater always called Jessie "Mama."

No, Robin! No!

Crafty Mary Ann knew just how to keep her friend Robin from gnawing on the itchy stitches from her lady surgery.

When I Grow Up, I Want to Be the Person Responsible for Succeeding So That My Parents Will Feel Less Uncomfortable with All of Their Failures

Ahh, nothing says football season like baby traction fan pants—not even fake fall leaves, emasculating ponchos, or generic banners on a stick.

"What's that, Marge? You say you got little Susie a new State cheerleading skirt? *Ha!* That's nothing! We have managed to swaddle our toddler entirely in the blazing colors of State, our glorious alma mater. Our child is the most enthusiastic fan under three feet that State has ever seen. And that's not all! Eighteen years from now, it will be our child who leads State to glorious victory. We already see the signs. If we throw him a football, he almost catches it. He's only 11 months old! OK, well, he doesn't so much 'almost catch it' as 'let it hit him in the face,' but he doesn't cry. That's right, he doesn't even cry. He's tough. He's a warrior! But right now I've gotta go, 'cause our little warrior has made a poopsie."

Crafts

Crochet Lives Forever in Our Hearts. And Unfortunately, Also in Our Homes.

We would be remiss if we didn't dedicate a section of this book to all the other handicrafts that have cluttered up the aforementioned decades.

In the '40s, American women were dealing with the war and the shortages that it brought on. They had to be inventive, making the things that they normally would buy. There is no greater (or sadder) example of this than the 1942 classic "Gift Shopping with Crochet," a little booklet that allows the crafter to *pretend* that making your own gifts is just as fun as hitting the local Woolworth's for a few hours. Why, who would want nice store-bought earrings when you can simply *crochet your own?*

Crafts improved slightly by the 1950s, if for no other reason than that the war was over—you didn't *have* to make everything yourself. But, of course, if you were a *good mother,* you still did anyway, so the 1950s were full of patterns for baby knitwear, baby blankets, baby hats, baby booties, baby toys, and crocheted babies for those women who don't have actual babies. What the heck? Oh, right . . . *the baby boom.*

The '60s and '70s weren't just the Age of Aquarius, they were also the Age of Macramé. And brother, that stuff was everywhere.

> ♪ *Harmony and understanding . . .*
> *plant hangers and owls abounding!*
> *No more store-bought derisions . . .*
> *knotted and beaded dreams of visions!*
> *Mystic crafting revelation!*
> *And the hanging plant's true liberation . . .*
> *Macramé!*
> *Maaaacraaameeé!* ♪

Onward to the 1980s, when we were all living in a material world and we were all material girls (and boys) . . . and yet we foolishly continued to *make* material possessions instead of just buying them at the mall like normal people. Looking through the '80s, you realize that some things just never change—war or peace, good economy or bad, *American Bandstand* or MTV, people *will just not let up with the damn crochet.*

And on that note, everyone please pull your reading glasses out of your crocheted cases, set your cocktail on a nice crocheted coaster, and *let us begin!*

An Evening of Pretend Shopping with Crochet

BOOK No. 191

GIFT SHOPPING

with Crochet

PRICE 10 CENTS

Crochet your Gifts **THIS YEAR!**

Your friends love to get hand-made gifts . . . (shows you've taken time, trouble and thought!). It's so e-a-s-y to crochet, and so inexpensive! Here's a book chock-full of darling gift ideas for dates all around the calendar . . . summer or winter, birthdays or anniversaries. . . .

Remember, there's nothing more appreciated than a hand-made gift! *So relax and crochet today,* for YOURSELF . . . for YOUR FRIENDS!

Ah, gift shopping with cro-chet! Well . . . it's not so much "shopping" as it is "sitting at home crocheting until your hands bleed to make gifts for friends who likely won't appreciate them anyway and they'll just wind up shoved in the back of a drawer behind some unopened boxes of decorative soaps."

But yes, "shopping" *does* make it sound more fun!

Crochet Earrings

Fun for Your Money!

MATERIALS for No. 2639
J. & P. COATS TATTING COTTON, 1 ball.
Steel crochet hook No. 14.
2 earring bases.
Continued on page 20

MATERIALS
for No. 2644
CLARK'S O.N.T. "BRILLIANT,"
1 ball of any self-shading or
variegated color. Steel crochet hook
No. 10, 2 earring bases.
Continued on page 20

MATERIALS for No. 2645
CLARK'S O.N.T. or J. & P. COATS
BEST SIX CORD MERCERIZED
CROCHET, size 30, 1 ball of any
color.
CLARK'S O.N.T. or J. & P. COATS
SIX STRAND EMBROIDERY FLOSS,
1 skein each of 2 contrasting colors.
Steel crochet hook No. 10,
2 earring bases.
Cont. on page 20

Flowerettes
No. 2639
Page 20

Bells No. 2644
Page 20

Buttons
No. 2645
Page 20

Okay, we're sitting in our most comfortable chair. We have our basket full of yarn and our best crochet hooks. We've got a teeny tiny little glass of sherry to *sip* while we work. We're all ready to "shop"! (So to speak.)

We'll start out with a little something for all the girls in the neighborhood—crocheted earrings. You *can too* crochet earrings, don't look at me like that! They're going to look lovely . . . just . . . lovely.

Gosh, that first glass of sherry went down awful fast. Maybe we shoulda used a bigger glass. Well, one more *schmall* glass won't hurt. . . .

MATERIALS:

CLARK'S O.N.T. COTTON RUG YARN, 4 balls of main color for Body (Yellow, Cream or Ecru); 1 ball of Brown for Hair.

CLARK'S O.N.T. or J. & P. COATS SIX STRAND EMBROIDERY FLOSS, 1 skein each of Red, Blue and Brown.

CLARK'S O.N.T. RUG and AFGHAN HOOK, size G.

Steel crochet hook No. 7.

½ yard printed cotton percale, 36 inches wide.

1 yard narrow ribbon.

Cotton batting.

GAUGE: 3 sts make 1 inch; 3 rnds make 1 inch.

HEAD . . . Starting at top with main color and G hook, ch 22. 1st rnd: Sc in 2nd ch from hook and in each ch across. Then working along opposite side of foundation chain, make sc in each ch across (42 sts around). Do not join rnds but work sc in each st around until piece measures 7 inches. Fasten off.

BODY . . . Starting at bottom with main color, ch 29. Work as for Head (56 sts around) until piece measures 11 inches. Fasten off.

ARM (Make 2) . . . Starting at top with main color, ch 9 and work as for Head (16 sts around) until piece measures 9 inches. Fasten off.

LEG (Make 2) . . . Work as for Arms for 10 inches. Fasten off. Stuff Head and Body with cotton batting. Run a draw string around opening and draw in slightly for neck. Sew Head to open end of Body, having Body extend beyond Head on both sides for shoulders. Stuff Arms and Legs and sew in place on Body.

EYE (Make 2) . . . With Blue Six Strand and No. 7 hook, ch 2. 1st rnd: 7 sc in 2nd ch from hook. Do not join rnds. 2nd rnd: 2 sc in each sc around (14 sts). 3rd rnd: * Sc in next sc, 2 sc in next sc. Repeat from * around (21 sts). Fasten off.

LOWER LIP . . . With Red ch 8; sc in 2nd ch from hook, h dc in next, dc in next, tr in next, dc in next, h dc in next, sc in next. Fasten off.

UPPER LIP . . . Ch 10, sc in 2nd ch from hook, h dc in next, dc in next, (tr in next) twice; dc in next, h dc in next, sc in next. Fasten off.

BANGS . . . Wind Brown Rug Yarn flatly over width of a piece of paper 1 inch wide and 6 inches long. Machine stitch 2 or 3 times along one edge. Tear out paper. Then cut one thickness of Rug Yarn close to stitching thus making Bangs 2 inches long. Sew in place across top of Head.

HAIR . . . Cut remainder of Brown Rug Yarn into 1-yard lengths. Lay them side by side to cover a 6 x 36-inch area. Machine stitch them together down middle (stitching should measure 6 inches), having 18-inch strands on each side of stitching. Place Hair on Head, one end of machine stitching in center of Bangs, remainder of stitching down back of Head. Sew securely to Head. Drape Hair over back of Head and across top of Bangs. Fasten strands close to Head at ends of Bangs. Make 2 braids and tie ends with ribbon. Tack braids in place. Sew Eyes and Mouth in place. Make eyelashes with Brown.

DRESS . . . Fold material in half making a double piece 18 x 18 inches. Make a slit along center 12 inches of fold. Turn under fabric around slit and sew in place, being sure a draw string can be run through (this is neck opening). Measuring 4½ inches down from fold, make a 7-inch slit parallel with fold through both thicknesses. Make a similar slit on other side. Sew top edges of this slit together for 3½ inches (sleeves). Make hem on sleeves wide enough for draw string. Sew side seams in to fit body of dress and sew in place. Use main color hem at bottom of skirt. Make a 2-inch Rug Yarn for draw strings at neck and sleeves. Braid remainder of main color Rug Yarn for sash.

· 9 ·

Okay . . . earrings are done. Well, we guess they're done. They still look sort of . . . odd . . . but we can't figure out what else to do to 'em. Oh well, stick a fork in those earrings—they're DONE!

Hee!

Moving on to our little niece Betsy . . . for Betsy it has to be a doll. But not some cold, plastic, store-bought doll. *Noooooooo.* We're gonna whip up little Jiffy Ann, the only 28-inch-tall toy with serial-killer handwriting.

"HELLO, MY NAME IS JIFFY ANN. I'M 28″ TALL. YOU REALLY DON'T WANT TO FALL ASLEEP WITH ME IN THE ROOM. OH, AND HIDE THE KNIVES FROM ME, OKAY?"

Yep, Jiffy Ann is creepy as hell, but maybe Little Betsy won't notice. Her eyesight isn't so great anyway.

Which reminds us—*where's the sherry bottle?*

Whoops! There is it! Now . . . just a leeeetle bit more in the glash and we'll get started on our next project—some darling crochet accessories for all the women in the family.

Lesh see . . . there's a giant lace collar for Grandma . . . a lapel flower for Aunt Martha . . . some weird long frilly thing for Cousin Ethel, who we don't like much anyway . . . and a bunch of oversized butterflies for dear old Ma, who enjoys oversized insect lapel pins. Probably.

And now . . . more sher-rrrrrrry! Gah, wish we could crochet another bottle.

Okeydokey . . . we alsho need something for sister Sue, the bestsh friend a girl could ever have. For Sue, it's a gonna be a Soft Handbag . . . a spechial object that is somehow both soft and "crunchy." Good old Shue'll love it!

Soft Handbag 15" long
No. 2638

MATERIALS:
J. & P. COATS KNIT-CRO-SHEEN,
3 balls of White or Ecru, or 5 balls of any color.
Steel crochet hook No. 1/0 (zero).
½ yard satin lining material.
A 10-inch zipper.

GAUGE: 13 sts make 2 inches; 7 rows make 2 inches.
Starting at side edge with double thread, ch 158 to measure 24½ inches.
1st row: H dc in 3rd ch from hook, h dc in each ch across (156 sts). Ch 3, turn. **2nd row:** Insert hook in front loop of 1st st and pull loop through, * insert hook in front loop of next st and pull loop through, (thread over and draw through 2 loops) twice; ch 1 (a group st made). Insert hook in front loop of next st. Repeat from * across (78 group
Continued on page 21

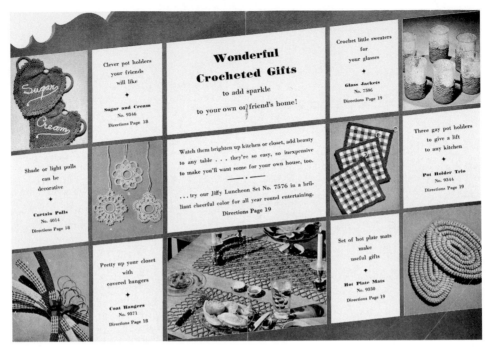

Lesh see . . . we got the earrings for all the girls, there's that terrifying doll for Little Betshy . . . Grandma getsh lace collar thing, flower for Martha, hideous lace frill for Ethel . . . *hic!* . . . butterflies for Ma . . . soft crunchy bag for Shue. But the booklet hash lotsa other gift ideas . . . did we leave anyone out?

What's this . . . *"Crochet little sweaters for your glasses"* . . . ?

Sweaters?

For our *glasses*?

For real?

Okay, yesh, we've been hitting the bottle just a little this evening, but are they actually implying that *we need to make homemade gifts for our kitchenware*? Because the sweaters for our glasses, thatsh one thing, but if that damn teakettle thinks she's getting some crocheted earrings . . . *well,* she's got another think coming!

Face Mask™ Is Especially Frightening When Used on a Decapitated Head!

Presenting Face Mask™, *the mask of a thousand uses!*

- **Acne so bad you don't want to leave the house?** *Face Mask™ is there!*

- **Need to rob a bank, liquor store, or house without being recognized?** *This is a job for . . . Face Mask™!*

- **Want help scaring an ex-girlfriend?** *It's Face Mask™ time!*

No. 841 FACE MASK

Fun Mask
(WILL FIT ALL HEAD SIZES)

MATERIAL: Lady Galt 4 ply *kroy Sock and Sweater Yarn (Group B)**

Main Colour (MC) 2 1-oz balls

Contrast (CC) 1 1-oz ball

1 pair needles Size 9 **OR THE SIZE NEEDLES YOU REQUIRE TO KNIT TO THE TENSION GIVEN BELOW**

TENSION: 6½ sts = 1 inch

Also available in the extra-creepy junior-sized Fun Mask™ style . . . perfect for the youngest of muggers!

Face Mask™—*ask for it by name!*

"Oh! How Thoughtful of Me!"

Times were tough in 1942. Your best beau was away at war, you had to go work in the canned-soup factory, and that damned chocolate ration was about to kill you.

Saddest of all, with no suitors around, you were reduced to *crocheting your own bouquet.* Sure, you tried to put on a happy face and pretend it was the same as a fresh bunch of roses delivered from Petersons Florist.

But it wasn't the same . . . it just wasn't the same.

CARNATION No. 4016

POPPY No. 4017 Page 22

DAISY No. 4019 Page 23

PINEAPPLE BASKET No. 9343 . . . Page 14

Crochet your own Bouquet!

Carnation No. 4016

MATERIALS:
CLARK'S O.N.T. "BRILLIANT," 3 balls.
Steel crochet hook No. 10.
A piece of heavy flower wire, 18 inches long.
Artificial carnation leaves and calyx.
Green rubberized tape.

Starting at base of carnation, ch 5. Join with sl st to form ring. **1st rnd:** Ch 3, 13 dc in ring. Join with sl st in top st of ch-3. **2nd and 3rd rnds:** Ch 3, dc in each dc around. Join. **4th rnd:** Ch 4, * dc in next dc, ch 1. Repeat from * around. Join. **5th to 9th rnds incl:** Ch 4, * dc in next sp, ch 1, dc in next dc, ch 1. Repeat from * around. Join. **10th rnd:** * Sc in next sp, ch 3, in next sp make 6 tr with p's between— to make a p, ch 3, sc in 3rd ch from hook; ch 3. Repeat from * around. Sl st in 1st sc made. Fasten off.

FINISHING . . . Fasten heavy wire securely to base of carnation. Slip calyx onto stem and push up close to petals, having slipped base inside calyx. Wind stem with rubberized tape, inserting leaves at desired intervals.

•15•

Dish Distracters

Do you prepare food that is truly disgusting?

Do your meals combine shrimp, toast triangles, and ice cream in a single dish? Does your recipe for a good casserole start with tomatoes and yellow mustard?

And finally, do you dislike the smell of your own burning flesh?

Then Threadbared Home has the answer!

New and Improved* Threadbared Hypnotizing Potholders!

At first glance, these appear to simply be hideously patterned potholders that keep your hands from getting singed as you remove your potluck poison from the oven. But look! If you use them when serving, too, they'll distract your guests from the edible excrement on the table! And that's not all! If you speak in a soothing voice and spin the Hypnotizing Potholders in a clockwise direction while your guests look directly at them, you can actually *hypnotize* your dinner guests, and they'll leave raving about your Ice Milk Étrouffée and Tomustard Casserole! They'll ask for the recipes and share them with their friends. They'll do pretty much anything you tell them to!** Threadbared Hypnotizing Potholders, perfect for terrible cooks everywhere.

*Threadbared Hypnotizing Potholders are actually unimproved. But that just doesn't have the same ring to it.

**Threadbared Home Inc. does not encourage the use of Threadbared Hypnotizing Potholders to dupe guests into publicly humiliating themselves or performing lewd sex acts. We will, however, accept pictures of said acts. Please mail them to our corporate office in a plain brown wrapper, c/o Mary & Kimberly.

One of These Things Is Not Like the Others

Recently, we were flipping through the pages of a "Knitwear for Infants" booklet and noticed something rather peculiar. While most of the children are certainly cute (though some are a bit large for babies; what were they *feeding* them back in the '60s?) . . . there was one particular child that stood out from the others.

Let's take a look, shall we?

Cute.

Cute.

Cute.

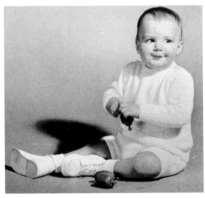
Cute.

Cute.

Um.

Exactly *what* is going on here?

Is it a . . .

Hideously disfigured Elephant Man baby?

Victim of its mother's overzealous crocheting habits?

Misfortunate child of extremist Ku Klux Klan members?

Still, whatever the terrible reason for enveloping your baby in needlework, one can't help but admire the handiwork that went into the detailed lacy edging. Nice, very nice.

Sometimes You Really Have to Ask Yourselves the Tough Questions

We're going with *not*.

There's Enough Macramé for Everyone!

So what's the perfect gift for a friend who's recently had a baby?

A cute stuffed animal?

A sweet little outfit?

A sterling-silver rattle?

Nah!

It's a *macramé hanging planter*!

Here we present the delightful "Kiddie Karousel," a charming little number that you can hang in a nursery. Sure to delight any tot!

Kiddie Karousel—Because It's Never Too Early to Start Them on Macramé Planters.

Kiddie Karousel

You need a little gift for your neighbor, the hippie across the street who always keeps your cats when you go on vacation. She's such a sweetheart, even if Fluffy and Bootsie always come home with their fur smelling like dope.

She'll like something earthy, bohemian . . . maybe even mystical.

Only Chyme Tyme will do.

Chyme Tyme

Ring - A - Ringer

Your swinging bachelor brother George just got a new "pad" and it's time to whip up a housewarming gift. The Ring-A-Ringer sounds like one of those awful sexual positions he always starts talking about at Christmas after a few too many eggnogs.

The Ring-A-Ringer.

Yes, he'll probably like that.

Don't worry—we haven't left the elder generation out of this Macramé Madness!

Yes, won't Grandmother be delighted when presented with this charming piece to hang on the wall of her industrial loft, cave, adobe hut, or whatever the hell she's living in that has walls like these?

And look, the grandchildren look even more adorable when surrounded by knotted pumpkin-colored yarn, don't they?

Grandmother's Delight

Black Beauty

Last but certainly not least, this planter is both a decorative object and a tool for bridging the social gap with that new biracial couple that moved into the neighborhood last month.

Let everyone know that you think "Black Is Beautiful" when you proudly march over to their house carrying this baby. Heck, it's 1975 and you're just as progressive as the next person. Plus, won't Martha Boatwright be jealous when you tell her that you got to see what their living room looks like?

So you see, young or old, straight or stoned, black or white—*there's a special macramé for everyone!* And remember, the more macramé you give away, the less of this crap you have to keep in your own house.

Allison and the Ape, Sitting in a Tree

A llison had known Jerry almost all her life and she really did care about him. Part of her even wished that she could feel for him the way he felt for her. After all, he was smart and funny, and he really had a good heart. But the whole "I scoot around on my knuckles like an ape" thing was kind of, well, embarrassing. What could Allison do? She found it difficult to be honest with him, especially when he was always showing up at her house with bananas.

The 1968 Reunion

Ah yes, never are the times so jolly as when the whole family gathers for fun, togetherness, and the wearing of ugly-ass hats.

The Chosen One

It started out as an innocent purchase from the County Craft Fair. Peggy was walking past a booth when it caught her eye. It seemed to be calling out to her, *"I choose you. I choose you. You . . . are . . . the Chosen One."*

She ignored it and went to the funnel cake stand.

On the way back to her car she passed the booth again, and once more, the crochet necklace beckoned to her: *"Choooooooosen One."*

She felt she had no option but to buy it. That whole hippie look wasn't really her thing, but maybe it would look OK with a turtleneck or something.

That was five months ago, and Peggy hasn't taken the necklace off since. The first time she tried, she felt a tightening around her collar and a burning sensation between her breasts. She had no choice.

She had to submit.

Peggy quit her job as a dental hygienist and spent her days building an aluminum foil tower in her backyard. She had to do everything the necklace told her to do.

Sometimes Peggy had fantasies about taking the garden shears to the necklace and ending it all. But she was scared—too scared to even try it. It had control now, and someday soon the mother ship would come and take them both away.

There was nothing left to do but wait.

Attack of the Killer Rugs

There will come a time when the rugs of the world will no longer be content to lie around on the floor, letting us walk all over them. They will grow weary of collecting our coffee-drip stains and our cat hair. They will rise up and turn against us with a vengeance the likes of which the craft world has never seen.

No one will escape. No one will be safe.

Crochet A Shag Rug by *Lady Galt*

Photographed at Gray Rocks Inn, St. Jovite, Mt. Tremblant, Quebec.

New from Lady Galt, Crocheted Shag Rugs. Simple to do, easy to follow instructions. No special equipment or canvas backing required. Your crochet hook and Lady Galt Sportsman Craft Yarn and you are ready to start creating.

Leaflet 1030 - .50c

Not even in the woods!

Crochet A Rug by *Lady Galt*

Photographed at Gray Rocks Inn, St. Jovite, Mt. Tremblant, Quebec.

New from Lady Galt, Crocheted Rugs. Simple to do, easy to follow instructions. No special equipment or canvas backing required. Your crochet hook and Lady Galt Sportsman Craft Yarn and you are ready to start creating.

Leaflet 1027 - .50c

Or by the lake!

KNIT A RUG by *Lady Galt*®

Photographed at Gray Rocks Inn, St. Jovite, Mt. Tremblant, Quebec.

New from Lady Galt, Hand Knit Rugs. Simple to do, easy to follow instructions. No special equipment or canvas backing required. Your knitting needles and Lady Galt Sportsman Craft Yarn and you are ready to start creating.

Leaflet 1023 - .50c

Not even on the dock!

Crochet A Rug
Crochet A Cushion
by *Lady Galt*

New from Lady Galt, Crocheted Rugs. Simple to do, easy to follow instructions. No special equipment or canvas backing required. Your crochet hook and Lady Galt Sportsman Craft Yarn and you are ready to start creating.

Leaflet 1022 - .50c

Or at the beach!

Crochet A Shag Rug
Crochet A Wall Hanging by *Lady Galt*

Photographed at Gray Rocks Inn, St. Jovite, Mt. Trembl

New from Lady Galt, Crocheted Rugs. Simple to do, easy to follow instructions. No special equipment or canvas backing required. Your crochet hook and Lady Galt Sportsman Craft Yarn and you are ready to start creating.

Leaflet 1024 - .50c

Crochet A Shag Rug by *Lady Galt*

Photographed at Gray Rocks Inn, St. Jovite, Mt. Tremblant, Quebec.

New from Lady Galt, Crocheted Shag Rugs. Simple to do, easy to follow instructions. No special equipment or canvas backing required. Your crochet hook and Lady Galt Sportsman Craft Yarn and you are ready to start creating.

Leaflet 1029 - .50c

Or up a tree!

Crochet A Rug by *Lady Galt*

New from Lady Galt, Crocheted Rugs. Simple to do, easy to follow instructions. No special equipment or canvas backing required. Your crochet hook and Lady Galt Sportsman Craft Yarn and you are ready to start creating.

Leaflet 1025 - .50c

Even people on trains in Canada will be unable to escape the horror!

My God, they can even climb mountains . . . and steps! Run, people, *run!*

Attack of the Killer Rugs—coming this fall to a theater near you.

Oh Yes, It's a Body Bag

Yes, why not on the terrace? In fact, why not use the afghan to transport the body of the pattern model you just killed and left on your terrace? That condescending, insensitive pattern model who had the nerve to wear a turban on the horse-and-buggy ride that you took together in Cairo . . . the same model who later said she only dates *real* photographers. Of course, she said that only *after* she had finished the entire plate of basboussa that *you* paid for. Be sure to lay her on the attractive multicolored crochet flower portion of the afghan in order to help hide the bloodstains . . . everyone will *not* find bloodstains original and beautiful.

DECORATION

oh yes, it's an afghan

This big, attractive, multicolored afghan, which everyone will find original and beautiful, can be used on a bed or a sofa, across the seats of a car, and why not on the terrace.

62 • The multicolored flowers blend easily with those in off-white to make this colonial style afghan. The two sizes of flowers are made in **crochet** and joined together as the work proceeds (Sport weight yarn).

48

Gullvägnr Is a Great Guy, but He Needs to Quit Asking if the Ladies Would Like to See His "Swedish Mëatbålls"

When Gullvägnr Sigürthsson first moved to the Meadowbrook subdivision in Dayton, Ohio, his neighbors weren't sure what to think. He was tall and strange and he carried a strong odor of damp wool. But then the Woodruff family over on Dogwood Circle invited Gullvägnr to their annual Christmas Open House. And who would have thought—he was the hit of the party!

Things hadn't started out so smoothly, though. Gullvägnr had burst into the front door, asking if everyone was *klar å parti* ("ready to party"), making old Fred Bailey spit right into his wassail.

But then Gullvägnr told his hostess that he had been a bartender back in his native land and he would be more than happy to whip up some drinks to get the crowd in the party spirit. Well, Barbara Woodruff has never been able to say no to anyone, so she led Gullvägnr into the rumpus room and told him to knock himself out.

The last party guest crawled out of the Woodruff home sometime around 4:30 P.M. the following Tuesday. Gullvägnr's signature drinks had provided enough social lubrication to grease the whole neighborhood and then some. Every-one forgot about Gullvägnr's woolly smell after throwing back a couple of these cocktails:

- ♥ Kinky Helsinki
- ♥ Läpp Dancer (special drink for lädies only!)
- ♥ Bjorn to Be Wild
- ♥ Dyslexic Tobogganist
- ♥ Hörny Viking ("Er that en löngboat in me trousers or åm I just happy to see you? HÄR HÄR HÄR!")
- ♥ Hërringtini (not for the faint of heart)
- ♥ Sven Göran Erickson Sventini (As Gull-vägnr always says, "When the Göran gets tough, he feels like a Näncy! HÄH!")
- ♥ Näked in Copenhägen
- ♥ Hërdy Gïrdy Bïrdy Gïrdy Bïrdy (on the röcks or neät)

Now no one in the neighborhood can *wait* for New Year's Eve.

Look at My New Purse. Moi Made It Moi Self.

She may have looked like a sweet girl with a quirky fashion sense and perky ponytails, but below that dimpled grin lay a festering darkness. No one knew how to get through to her. The counselors at juvie hall could only pray that the photos of Kermie and Grover lying furless in that alley would help her realize the gravity of what she had done. And there were at least three other colors of fur on that purse. God only knew where those bodies were.

All the Señoritas Go Loco for Macramé

Ooooh, "Macramé Hacienda"! *Cha-cha-cha!* Finally, we're in for something a little different, something a little spicier than your usual white-bread macramé. Something bold and ethnic and *exciting*! Something with a little South-of-the-Border flair! Let's open up and take a look!

"Poncho"

"Sancho"

"Pedro"

What in the inferno is this?

This isn't *spicy*! This isn't *inspired*!

This is just a stupid macramé bear, a poodle, and a damned turtle. The only difference here is that instead of being named "Teddy, Fifi, and Pokey," they're called "Sancho, Poncho, and Pedro."

I'm starting to get the terrible feeling that we've been had. Well, no one is going to pull the wool over my *ojos*. But maybe it gets better . . .

"Su Casa"

"Su Casa"? You've got to be kidding me! How 'bout a little creativity? A little originality?

Perhaps *"Place mats y coasters de costa de la puesta del sol"* ("Place mats and coasters of the sunset"), or maybe *"Accesories de macramé para la cocina"* ("Macramé accessories for the kitchen"—a little boring, yes, but God, it's still better than "Su Casa"), or possibly *"Artículos de mesa alegres que son vago hispánicos en naturaleza"* ("Cheerful tableware that is vaguely Hispanic in nature")?

There, we just dashed off three alternate names in about forty-five seconds. Perhaps the booklet's author should head back to "Su Casa" and think a little harder.

"el Luz"

And now we have this lovely little lamp shade, which is guaranteed to burst into flames the second it accidentally makes contact with an exposed bulb.

Its name? Why, it's "The Light," of course! Who here is surprised?

Let's move right along to the "Ojo de Dios." It may appear to be a large macramé kite, but the "Eyes of God" is actually a traditional Mexican ornament thought to ward off evil spirits. Rest assured that your pottery vase and jar of wheat will go unharmed with this handmade monstrosity lording over them.

There's nothing really wrong with the name "Ojo de Dios," since this is the authentic Spanish title. Still, we worked ourselves up into such a froth over this booklet's previous transgressions that we continue to feel slightly irked, as though the author has cheated somehow by using the traditional name.

"Ojo de Dios"

"Siesta"

"Siesta" - "Dos"

"Siesta" - "Tres"

"Siesta" - "Uno"

And finally, we round things out with this trio of cheery pillows named "Siesta."

There's "Siesta Uno, Siesta Dos, and Siesta Tres." That's "One, Two, and Three" for those philistines not well-versed in the Spanish language.

Yes, this truly was a veritable Hacienda of Macramé. Suddenly, we feel the need for a large shot of tequila and a long siesta.

AfghaniTan

It seemed like a funny prank. The girls at the sorority house decided to slip Meg a roofie and leave her pinned to the ground using some drywall nails and their housemother's favorite afghan. They figured she'd wake up, struggle to get out, and have to walk back to campus. Maybe that would teach her a lesson. You couldn't just steal your roomie's last Ho-Ho and her date to the Kappa Sig mixer all in one week and expect to get away with it!

What they didn't count on was the kick-ass crochet tan she'd have when she finally came to and shimmied her way out of the spread. The boys went wild for it, and soon girls could be seen lying all over campus covered in bikinis and afghans.

Leaflet 1038 / 50c

Lady Galt®

Bedspread

Crochet Pinwheel Bedspread
featured in machine launderable
Lady Galt double knitting/knitting
worsted Sayelle* yarn
Traduction française des abréviations incluses

Frankly, We're Most Unnerved by the Way He Stares at You While You're on the Toilet

KING KROKER *the Frog*

Greetings! I am King Kroker, Crocheted Amphibian Lord of the Bathroom! I would be charmed to assist you in your toilette!

Care to wash your hands? I've a bar of soap for you right here . . . all you have to do is remove it from my tongue.

Hand towel? You can use the one dangling from my feet. That's right, get those hands nice and dry.

Washcloth? Why, there's one here in my lap! Yes, frogs have laps, too. That's right . . . take the washcloth . . . go ahead. Your face looks dirty . . . I think you should wash it. I've got a washcloth . . . right here . . . in my lap . . . just for you. A little washcloth . . . for you to rub . . . all over your face. Go ahead . . . go on. *For God's sake* . . . TAKE THE WASHCLOTH!

Animal Farm, Circa 1982

Kill me now.

Sometimes crochet can go sort of . . . *wrong.*

Sure, the little girl looks vaguely happy, but did you take a look at the puppets' *faces*?

Something isn't right here.

Dear God. Why me?

Hand up my ass, eh? Hmmm . . . not bad.

Acknowledgments

We would like to thank Caroline Greeven and Marc Gerald with the Agency Group for finding us and making all kinds of great things happen.

Lindsey Moore and Carrie Thornton with the Crown Publishing Group for their support, creative input, and for generously answering our multitudes of questions.

All of our friends and families, but in particular our parents—Deigie and Otis Andrews and Judy and Steve Harris. Thank you for raising us to be nice girls. Please ignore all the gratuitous cursing in this book.

And last but certainly not least, we would like to thank our husbands—Alan Wrenn and Andrew Watkins—for supporting us, introducing us to each other, and generally just putting up with us during the year it took to create this book.

About the Authors

KIMBERLY WRENN lives outside of Atlanta with her husband, Alan. She has a Ph.D. in industrial/organizational psychology, spending her days as a mild-mannered psychologist and her nights as an Internet smarty-pants.

MARY WATKINS is a native of Georgia and also lives just outside of Atlanta with her husband, Andrew. A former marketing manager, she now spends her days as a writer and a somewhat lazy housewife.

Together, Mary and Kimberly run the popular website Threadbared.com.

Credits